Fighting For Excellence
in Leadership

Fighting For Excellence in Leadership

by Casey Treat

Published by

Christian Faith Center
P.O. Box 98800
Seattle, WA 98198

Contents

Introduction

From the beginning of time, people have had to fight for what is good and right. This is a reality that will continue on in human history until we enter into the presence of the Lord.

Even the very first man and woman were confronted with this fight. In Genesis chapter three, the enemy came to take what belonged to Adam and Eve. He came in with deception and subtlety. Unfortunately, they did not fight properly and lost that battle. This caused them to spend the rest of their lives fighting to regain what had been taken from them.

Throughout the entire Bible, from that first battle between Adam, Eve, and the serpent, we see that it is a Book of battles. From Genesis through Revelation we find war after war after war. It is time that we recognize and accept the fact that fighting for what is good and right should be a part of *our* lives as well.

Abraham had to fight for Lot, his family, his friends and his relatives. He fought for his faith in God and the covenant that God had promised to him.

Moses fought to deliver his people, Israel, from Egypt. He fought to lead his people through the struggles of the wilderness. He brought them to the edge of the Promised Land, and even though it was promised to them by God, they still had to fight before they could possess it.

Gideon had to fight. His first battle was to see himself as God saw him. His self-image was so low that he had to fight to see himself as a mighty man of valor. Once he had gained that victory, he began to rally the troops to convince the nation they could overthrow the Midianites. They fought for the freedom of their nation.

David fought for the people of Israel to overcome the Philistines and others who would try to dominate their land. The greatest king of Israel was great because of his fighting spirit.

Jesus had to fight. He fought the Pharisees, the Sadducees and the religious traditions of His day. He fought sickness, demons and poverty. When He died, He went to hell and fought Satan himself! The Bible says He made an open show of the devil, stripped him of all of his power, triumphing over him in the cross. Jesus will come back as King of Kings and Lord of Lords with a sharp, two-edged sword in His hand. A victorious conqueror, a soldier and a fighter, Jesus is the Captain of our salvation!

As we move on through history, we see how Martin Luther fought against the religious traditions of men. His whole life was a battle to bring faith back to the church.

John Wesley fought against the traditions of church and state. He fought against the apathy of a world that was dying and going to hell. He fought for holiness and revival to change the course of our world.

Early Pentecostal believers had to fight for the right to pray in tongues and have a church building.

In a much more physical way, some of our own parents and grandparents fought in world wars so that we could have a free country. They fought and gave their lives so people would not live under the control of guns and military powers.

We are here today because of the centuries of fighting that have gone on before us. All that we have, from the Bible to the nation in which we live, is ours because people were willing to fight!

<u>God is a God of war. The Bible is a Book of battles and the Christian life is a *fight of faith.*</u> Do we believe these truths are reality for our lives in this day and hour? Have we become soldiers in the army of the Lord?

I believe God is calling us, stirring us to fight for what is good, right and excellent. He is calling us to fight for the will of God in our lives, families, nation and our world. I believe it's the call of the Spirit to the Church. It's time to rise up. It's time to fight the good fight of faith!

1
The Spirit of War

"So Jesus answered and said to them, "Have faith in God.

For assuredly, I say to you, whoever says to this mountain, 'Be removed and be cast into the sea,' and does not doubt in his heart, but believes that those things he says will come to pass, he will have whatever he says.

Therefore I say to you, whatever things you ask when you pray, believe that you receive them, and you will have them."

Mark 11:22-24

Jesus said, "And from the days of John the Baptist until now the kingdom of heaven suffers violence, and the violent take it by force" (Matthew 11:12). When Jesus said "until now," I believe he was talking about "ad infinitum," from now on. He meant this church age—the age of grace. The *spirit* of the phrase, "the violent take it by force," coupled with faith that speaks to mountains, is essential if you want to walk with God today.

There was a time when we could just go to seminars, be consumed with study, and "wait on the Lord." We studied faith, tongues, salvation and debated doctrinal issues. But I believe the day of simply studying and learning the Word is gone. We need to continue to grow and have a "take it by force" faith if we want to successfully walk with God.

Many of us haven't realized that God's method and focus have changed. We have tried to figure out what He's doing by reading a commentary; but the Spirit of God won't be found in a commentary. It is with our faith that we accept what God is doing in *this day* and *this hour*. This is not the day for just *studying about faith*; this is the day for *using it*! Let's not only study about armor; let's put it on! Put God's Word into *action!* We must stop going through our old routines just doing what we're "supposed" to do. Let's stop *talking* about mountains and *move them* out of the way!

Pastors, stop talking about your cities, problems, hindrances, budgets and economy.

Stop talking about them and blow them out of the way! Conquer and take them by force! Fight until you see your vision come to pass!

Don't Wander — Possess!

We cannot sit around talking about "the way we were." We've come *out* of Egypt. We've been delivered from bondage—we're not slaves anymore. We have the blessing of God. We are walking with God and we know how to be led by the Spirit. Now we need to possess the Promised Land. We can't afford to get together to talk about how great it is to be out of Egypt. We need to start looking for some walls to tear down! *Let's possess the land! Let's overtake the enemy!*

We will never possess the Promised Land or receive the promises of God just by knowing *about* them. The children of Israel spied out the land and knew all about it. They looked it over and said, "It's great!" But they didn't possess it just by knowing about it. Some of us know so much but are not doing anything with our knowledge. We think if we keep studying that somehow the Promised Land will fall in our laps.

Some of us believe if we get another revelation, learn just a little more about church administration and receive some kind of divine insight, the Promised Land will be ours. But the truth is, it's time now to possess it! Possess what the scripture says is yours. *Just do it!* Go after it. Be violent and have a *take-it-by-force* spirit!

One of the saddest things for me to see is people who have gifts and talents...who have the potential to be great whether it's in business, music, ministry, or leadership...but don't have a violent spirit. They're stuck in a mediocre, lukewarm and maintenance frame of mind, and they will never be all that they could be. They wander around the wilderness talking about how good it is not to be in Egypt, but they never possess the Promised Land.

Matthew 11:12 in the Moffatt translation refers to storming the realm of heaven. Storming it? That doesn't sound very respectable. We need to be storming the kingdom of God, going after it and doing whatever we have to do to get it!

Some people will never fulfill this scripture because they are too nice. They won't storm the kingdom of God. Yes, they will have a nice church and a nice ministry, but they will never storm the kingdom of

God and take it by force. They are never going to possess the Promised Land!

The Amplified Bible says, **"And from the days of John the Baptist until the present time, the kingdom of heaven has endured violent assault, and violent men seize it by force [as a precious prize—a share in the heavenly kingdom is sought with most ardent zeal and intense exertion]"** (Matthew 11:12 Amplified). We need intense Christians.

Some people become nervous when they come to Christian Faith Center. When they try to tell me what they don't like about it, they might say, "Well, you know, it's kind of loud...well, it's not that it's loud, but...it's kind of fast. Well, it's not that it's fast...it's kind of young. Well, it's not all that young...."

I know what it is—*it's intense!* And it gets more intense everyday. We are ardently taking the kingdom by force! *We are intensely taking it by force, with ardent zeal and intense exertion!*

If you are not violent, you won't get the kingdom! If you want to sit around, you will not get it. The kingdom will pass you by.

You won't get it by just listening and watching. Violent people *take it by force with ardent zeal and intense exertion.*

The New International Version says, **"...forceful men lay hold of it" (Matthew 11:12 NIV).** What is a forceful person? It is someone who rubs us the wrong way sometimes. It's time we start rubbing the world the wrong way. *It's time we became forceful!*

What Do You Want?

To fight the fight of faith and take the kingdom by force, we must start by knowing what we want.

Think of the blind man in Mark 10:47-52 who cried out, **"Jesus, Son of David, have mercy on me!"** He knew what he wanted.

The people said to him, *"Be quiet! Don't be so loud. Don't be so wild. Don't be so forceful. Can't you be a little more respectable? Do you have to act like a wild man?"*

Then what did the blind man do? He cried out more! **"Jesus, Son of David, have mercy on me!"**

When Jesus heard him, He stopped and told the people to bring the man to Him.

Some preachers have whined, cried, bawled and squalled for years; yet Jesus has never stopped for them. But he stopped for this man because he was ardently, zealously, intensely crying out. Imagine this blind man being led to where Jesus was waiting. He was obviously blind, yet Jesus asked him, **"What do you want?"**

The blind man said, **"I want to see."**

Jesus said, **"Your faith has made you whole."** Immediately he received his sight!

Some of us have *little* prayer requests that deal with making it through the month, getting the budget met for the year, or getting the building finished. Is that really all we want? That may be all we will get because we've never told God what we *really* want!

I'm telling God what I want! I want a church that's affecting the entire Northwest. I want a church that is doing the works of Jesus. I want a university that is developing leaders—men and women of God who are educated, who can really do something in our society. I don't want a little religious church; I want something powerful!

What do you want? Are you praying, "Thy will be done" and waiting for God to move? Fighting this fight means knowing what you want. Do you really know?

When my children start whining, I ask them, "What do you want?! Talk! Tell me what you want!"

God is asking us, *"What do you want?!"* Once you know what you want, go after it! Get violent, forceful and intense and go after your vision!

In Numbers chapter 13, we have the story of how the spies were sent out to survey the Promised Land. They all came back with an evil report except for two men. Here's what the Bible says about one of them. **"Then Caleb quieted the people before Moses, and said, 'Let us go up at once and take possession, for we are well able to overcome it" (Numbers 13:30).** He didn't want to talk about Egypt, or the pillar of cloud and the pillar of fire. He didn't want to talk about manna or how difficult it might be to move forward. He wanted to possess the land! Caleb had a violent, take-it-by-force attitude.

In Numbers 14:24 God said, **"But My servant Caleb, because he has a different spirit in him...."** Do you have a spirit like everyone around you or do you have another spirit? If you are going to possess the land, you had better have a different kind of spirit. That means a different spirit than some of the people in your congregation. If they aren't telling you to slow down and take it easy, then you are probably much like them.

You need a different spirit—one like that of Caleb. God said, **"But My servant Caleb...has followed Me fully..." (Numbers 14:24).** He didn't follow the crowd or do what was acceptable. *He followed God fully.* Verse 24 continues, **"...Caleb...I will bring into the land where he went, and his descendants shall inherit it."**

Because the children of Israel rejected what Caleb and Joshua had said, they wandered in the wilderness for forty years and suffered all kinds of misery. Finally, in Joshua 14 we read how the last "pillar" in the church—the last dry, old, stale, religious person—died. Then the people could finally go over into the Promised Land.

After they arrived in the Promised Land, we read:

> **"Then the children of Judah came to Joshua in Gilgal. And Caleb the son of Jephunneh the Kenizzite said to**

him: 'You know the word which the LORD said to Moses the man of God concerning you and me in Kadesh Barnea.

I was forty years old when Moses the servant of the LORD sent me from Kadesh Barnea to spy out the land, and I brought back word to him as it was in my heart."

Joshua 14:6-7

This spirit was in his heart. He had a different spirit; he was a violent man and this spirit was *in* him.

"Nevertheless my brethren who went up with me made the heart of the people melt, but I wholly followed the LORD my God.

So Moses swore on that day, saying, 'Surely the land where your foot has trodden shall be your inheritance and your children's forever, because you have wholly followed the LORD my God.'

And now, behold, the LORD has kept me alive, as He said, these forty-five years, ever since the LORD spoke this word to Moses while Israel wandered in the wilderness; and now, here I am this day, eighty-five years old.

As yet I am as strong this day as I was on the day that Moses sent me; just as my strength was then, so now is my strength for war, both for going out and for coming in."

Joshua 14:8-11

God has said that we, too, are strong through Christ who strengthens us. But many of us have not realized that strength because we're not at war—so we don't need it! We will never need much strength if we're not going to fight. Why do we have strength? To go to war and win!

In Joshua 14:12 we read, **"Now therefore, give me this mountain...."** Caleb knew what he wanted, and Joshua blessed him and told him to *go and get it*.

Do you know what you want? Are you willing to go to war for it? Are you willing to fight for it? Some of you are depressed because you've been thinking about all your enemies, your needs and your problems instead of going to war against them. Some of you are weak because you have been looking at the circumstances instead of overcoming them.

If you want to move with God today, it's not going to happen by putting on a convention or having a nice building. It's not the banquets, the speakers, or the television programs that will bring results. It's the violent, *take-it-by-force* attitude that says, "Whatever I've got to do, I'm going to do it!"

The book of Ecclesiastes says there is a time for peace and a time for war. There is a time for love and a time for hate. I hate what the devil is doing to our people and I'm ready to go to war against it! If you will get that same spirit, you will discover a greater ability than you have ever known before. Not a program, not a sermon, but a spirit—*a spirit of war.*

2
The Fight of Faith

"The LORD is my strength and
song, and He has become my salvation;
He is my God, and I will praise Him;
My father's God, and I will exalt Him.

The LORD is a man of war; the
LORD is His name."

Exodus 15:2-3

God leads His people in war because we
must fight for what is good and right.

In I Timothy 6:12, Paul teaches that we
are to fight the good fight of faith. Some of
us have come to the point where we believe
we are fighting because we don't have faith.
We believe if we had faith, there would be
no fight. But the Bible says *faith itself is a
fight!*

Faith is fighting for healing when
healing doesn't seem to be there. It's fighting
for prosperity when the money doesn't

seem to be there. It's fighting for peace in your home when it seems like everything is against you. *Faith is fighting.*

To believe that if you had the faith then there would be no fight is unscriptural. Having faith means you're willing to fight. The people who fight against the problems and the trials of life are not the ones with weak faith. They're the ones who have strong faith. The people who won't fight, who give up, who turn away, are the ones with weak faith.

Fighters are faith people. They're the ones who say, "No! I'm not going to let my marriage end in divorce. I'm going to fight for my family."

"No! I'm not going to let my child live in this sickness and this physical problem. I'm going to fight."

"No! I'm not going to let my church stagnate and become another bunch of pew warmers. I'm going to fight for the Spirit of God to move in my church. I'm going to fight with everything I have to change my world." That's the spirit of faith people.

"You therefore must endure hardship as a good soldier of Jesus Christ" (II Timothy 2:3).

Endure hardship! So many of us today shy away from hardship. If it's hard, it must not be the Lord! If it's hard, it can't be God's will. God is a God of war. He will not lead you into easiness, He will lead you into battle. The battle will be hard, but here's the exciting part: you will always win if you follow God!

The mentality of so many is to avoid hardness; to avoid the challenge of service to the Lord. We tend to want to avoid the challenge of commitment to the Lord, and the challenge of ministry and the giving of our lives.

Doing the will of God doesn't mean we go the easy way. It would be much easier for us to be content with our churches and the way they are now. Why build universities? Why have Christian schools? Why buy more property? Why believe God for more finances to help more people? Why start more daycares? The answer is because we're fighting a battle and whether it's hard or not is not the issue. We are commanded to endure hardness as good soldiers, and to go into all the world and make disciples.

There is an easier way. There's a "maintenance mentality" that comforts the flesh and soul. That mentality is believing that being saved and going to heaven is all that really counts.

There is a rest for the people of God; yet Paul tells us to *labor to enter into that rest* (Hebrews 4:11). The truth in this scripture is the fact that if we don't fight, we'll never have victory. If we never have victory, we'll never have peace. And if there is no peace, there is no real rest.

So how do you enter into the rest of the Lord? You fight until you win, then you enjoy your victory and take peace and comfort because the battle has been won. Then you get strengthened for the next battle. There is a rest, but it comes as we endure hardness. The fact that the going is difficult does not mean that you are out of the will of God. In fact it's probably a very good sign that you're in the will of God.

When we seek for that comfort, peace, and the easy way, we are probably running away from the battle into which God is calling us. Soldiers who run away from battle are not honored and they are not given medals. They are discharged. But soldiers who endure hardness are honored by their Lord and Master.

"No one engaged in warfare entangles himself with the affairs of this life, that he may please him who enlisted him as a soldier" (II Timothy 2:4). I want to please God. I want to stand before God and hear, "Well done, thou good and faithful soldier." I believe pleasing God is more important than getting my house paid off or getting my yard mowed. Now the lawn should be mowed, but when the yard, the house, the job and other things are more important than pleasing God as a soldier who endures hardness, then the priorities are wrong. Paul said to not be entangled with the affairs of life.

Not a Physical Wave

I want to make something very clear. I am not talking about a fleshly battle, or a soulish, emotional battle. *We do not war after the flesh.* In Ephesians 6:10-11, Paul says: **"Finally, my brethren, be strong in the Lord and in the power of His might. Put on the whole armor of God, that you may be able to stand against the wiles of the devil."**

Notice he didn't say to be strong so we can stand against our neighbors, our spouses, or our government. He said to stand against the wiles of the devil. We wrestle not against men, women, or flesh and blood. So against whom do we wrestle? Principalities, powers, rulers of the darkness, and spiritual wickedness in high places. That's who we're fighting. <u>It's a spiritual war, not a fleshly or emotional war.</u>

"For though we walk in the flesh, we do not war according to the flesh" (II Corinthians 10:3). Too often when we read or hear this message from scripture, we receive it as a heavy load or burden. We feel we need to perform more, do more, work harder and better. So instead of being encouraged and motivated in a positive way, we end up being discouraged and depressed. We relate to these scriptures in terms of warring after the flesh. Warring after the flesh becomes tiring and heavy, and we soon start feeling burned out and worn out. We have thoughts like, "Can I ever do enough?" That phrase is the key to let us know we've been fighting the wrong way.

Even as a pastor, I pray, study, preach, train and teach my staff, prepare the services, and spend time being taught. Yet there are still times I think, "Can I ever do enough, or be good enough for the church and the people to grow?"

If I hear that someone is upset and they don't like something I did, I take it personally and think things like, "How could I do that? That was so wrong. I need to think about what I'm doing; I need to be more responsible."

Then I realize what is happening: I've left the Spirit and I'm in the flesh. And warring after the flesh wears us out. We get tired and burned out, and soon we start talking about needing a vacation. We start talking about needing to find a church where the people love us. It is simply depressing to war "after the flesh."

Warring after the flesh causes us to think thoughts like, "I should have more faith. I need to get a better job so I can make more money. Then I can have a better car and I can show everybody I really have faith."

Warring after the flesh is comparing ourselves with other people. If our motives are for doing things so people will see and approve of us, we will burn out and be discouraged because we are warring after the flesh and not after the Spirit. We are trying to impress *them*, keep up with *them*, and show *them* our faith. This only brings failure. And with failure comes anger and discouragement. That's warring after the flesh. We're competing and comparing for the rewards of men or looking for a "pat on the back."

We do not war after the flesh. It's not of God. This is the way of the world: climbing the corporate ladder, trying to get two cars in the garage, trying to get our home to be as good as the neighbor's home. This kind of fighting is not the fight of faith. It's the fight of the flesh! This kind of fighting will wear us out and tear us down.

There is no such thing as "spiritual burn out." That term is a misnomer. It really can't happen. You cannot walk in the Spirit and burn out. You cannot fight in the Spirit and burn out. You cannot live a spiritual life and burn out. Your flesh can burn out, your soul can burn out, your emotions can burn out, your religious traditions can burn out. *But your spirit will never burn out!*

How *can* your spirit burn out? If your spirit is born of the Holy Spirit, joined as one to the Lord, receiving power from on high, how is your spirit going to burn out? If your spirit ever does burn out, it means that God burned out.

Jesus said His yoke is easy and His burden is light. If we're fighting a spiritual warfare, it may be hard. It may not be fun but we don't burn out. We stay on top and strong in the Lord. We don't get discouraged and burdened because *His yoke* is easy and *His burden* is light. It's the anointing of the Spirit that breaks the yoke of bondage. That anointing of the Spirit leads us into battle; therefore, we don't have to figure everything out and struggle emotionally and physically.

We do not fight for social status, or for acceptance or approval. We do not fight for earthly possessions or positions. We do not compare and compete with those around us. Those things shouldn't matter. We love one another and together we war in the Spirit. And that spiritual warfare is fought with faith, with the Word, with vision and prayer, with boldness and with love. These tools for warfare will not wear us out. They will not beat us down or make us feel inadequate.

If we will fight this fight with faith, with vision, prayer and boldness, we will have victory. We are in a spiritual fight, not a carnal fight. Don't accept it as a burden. Accept it as energizing our spiritual batteries and say, "Yes, I can endure hardness as a soldier of Jesus Christ. I can fight the good fight of faith. And I can have what God has destined for me."

3
Our Excellent God!

"O LORD, our Lord, how excellent is Your name in all the earth, You who set Your glory above the heavens!" (Psalm 8:1) How excellent is the Lord's name. Throughout the Bible, every person's name described his being, his person, and his character. When God changed Abram's name to Abraham, it was because his life had changed. When Jesus changed Simon's name to Peter, it was because his life was different. So when the Bible says God's name is excellent, it means He is an excellent Being. His character is excellent. His personality is excellent. Everything He does is excellent!

When God creates, He creates with excellence. Have you ever considered the world around us? It is excellent! When God provides salvation, it is excellent. It is total, complete, eternal salvation. As sons and daughters of God, we are commanded to be imitators of God (Ephesians 5:1). That means we are to follow Him and be like Him as much as we possibly can. That means we are excellent people. Everything we do and say is, or should be, excellent.

People should look at us and see that we are different. We shouldn't be like everyone else. When bad things happen, we shouldn't get depressed and discouraged. Our Father is excellent and we should be imitating Him. We haven't accomplished it yet, and we have a long way to go, but we should be seeking to be excellent. We fight for excellence in every realm of life.

"How excellent is thy lovingkindness, O God! Therefore, the children of men put their trust under the shadow of thy wings" (Psalm 36:7, KJV). He's so excellent that we can trust Him and stay with Him.

"You are more glorious and excellent than the mountains of prey" (Psalm 76:4). God is more excellent and glorious than anything on this earth!

"Let them praise the name of the Lord: for his name alone is excellent; his glory is above the earth and heaven" (Psalm 148:13, KJV). What kind of God do we serve? *An* *excellent God.* What kind of work does He do? *Excellent work.* How has He blessed us? *With excellence!*

"Praise Him for His mighty acts; praise Him according to His excellent greatness!" (Psalm 150:2) It's time for the church to fight for excellence in our walk with God. Let's fight to be excellent people; not mediocre, lukewarm, apathetic, religious people—but excellent people! This spirit of excellence will be our greatest evangelistic tool in the end times. I believe this will win more people to God than all the tracts we could print, or all the tapes we could duplicate.

If we as Christian leaders will begin to fight for excellence in everything we say and do, the world will know that we are different from the rest. They may not get too much out of our television shows, but our lifestyles will be excellent.

When we say Jehovah Rapha, we mean God the Healer. When we say Jehovah Jireh, we mean God the Provider. When we say Jehovah Tsidkenu, we mean God is Righteous. When we say Jehovah Nissi, we say God is our Banner. His name describes who He is. Everything He is, everything He does, everything He says is excellent.

Excellence is God, and God is always excellent. He's never mediocre. He's never second class or second rate. He's always *first* class. That's what God is all about.

His Name — Our Name

His name is excellent. Since we are His people called by His Name, we should be excellent people. That means everything we say and do, and our whole being should be excellent! When that happens, we will become light in this world! We will shine out from everyone else because the world's standard is not excellence.

Worldly people despise and fear excellence. They vote for politicians who will compromise because they don't want strong, excellent people. They want nice, compromising people who will pass laws that compromise. If they can't handle "sin," they legalize it. There is compromise in so many ways. Excellence is like turning on the lights in a darkened room—it is blinding!

Compromise can become so comfortable that we look for reasons not to fight. That way we don't have to stand for righteousness. Many Christians and many Christian leaders think it's okay to just go to a church where people don't have to do anything. The leaders don't challenge the people to praise God because they might get nervous and not come back. They aren't told to raise their hands and bless the Lord because they might leave and go to another church. They don't have people pray in the Spirit because they might not come anymore. But I believe there is a land full of people rising up with a new spirit. It's a spirit of excellence, and they are ready to fight for excellence in every area of life!

At Christian Faith Center, we have established a certain degree of excellence, and sometimes it makes people nervous. We have to break old traditions because in the past, the church has been known to be sloppy, unwise, carnal, and fighters over petty things. In fact, employers many times shy away from Christians because they're always wanting something for nothing. And they're some of the laziest workers. If our reputation was that of excellence, all we would have to do is walk into an interview and say, "I'm looking for a job. I'm a Christian and I'm filled with the Holy Spirit and pray in tongues every day."

"When can you go to work? We need people like you: honest, hard-working, loyal, and faithful. How soon can you start?" the employer would then eagerly ask. If we were excellent in all we did, everyone would want to hire a Christian! But we haven't been excellent. Instead we've been sloppy, lazy, and religious.

"The righteous is more excellent than his neighbor..." (Proverbs 12:26 KJV). Do your neighbors realize your relationship with God because of the excellence of your life? That doesn't just mean in the physical things, although if excellence is in you, it will be manifested through you. It's hard to preach how excellent your God is when your yard is one big weed. It's hard to preach about how excellent your God is, when your car is held together by Jesus bumper stickers. If it's in you, it's going to show in every area of your life. Our God, our Lord is excellent! He has an excellent name. If we belong to Him, then our name is excellent. Everything we do and say should reflect the excellent God whom we serve.

Taking a Stand for Excellence

Some time ago, something I had struggled with for years became very clear to me. When we first opened the church, I wanted to do everything right. I wanted to be the best I could be. I wanted to be a *real* pastor, not just a religious person going through some motions, putting on a show. I didn't want a bunch of people coming to church just because it was Sunday morning. I would work, pray, discipline myself, study, prepare, and do everything I could to help people and meet their needs.

As the staff grew, I would gather them together to teach and train them to discipline themselves. We would confront each other to be the best, the strongest, the most excellent we could be. We were pressing for excellence! People would come, listen and say, "We loved it! It was the greatest. It was just what we've been looking for." But then we would never see them again.

So I'd encourage the staff to be *more* excellent. The next week the same thing would happen again. I battled over the cause of this for a long time.

Then the Lord revealed to me this truth: the more excellence there is, the harder it is for people to relate to it. People will relate to weakness and mediocrity before they will relate to excellence. Only those who have a real desire for excellence will go through the changes necessary to make it a normal part of their lives. Most people don't want to hear about it; they want compromise instead of excellence.

Does that mean I should be sloppy so people will like me? Should I be a fool so everyone will think I'm cool? It is sad to think that people will relate to mediocrity and negativity before they will relate to excellence.

The Lord had to help me understand how to communicate excellence in a way in which people can understand and grow. It's not easy to have a standard of excellence. More people will dislike you than will like you for it.

In the Old Testament, Daniel fought for excellence and was despised by many. But in spite of that he rose to the top in the nation of Babylon and became the counselor to the king. Taking a stand for excellence isn't the most popular thing to do, but if we stay strong, we, too, will rise to the top like Daniel.

How Excellent Are You?

"And to the angel of the church of the Laodiceans write, 'These things says the Amen, the Faithful and True

Witness, the Beginning of the creation of God:

"I know your works, that you are neither cold nor hot. I could wish you were cold or hot.

So then, because you are lukewarm, and neither cold nor hot, I will spew you out of My mouth.

Because you say, 'I am rich, have become wealthy, and have need of nothing' —and do not know that you are wretched, miserable, poor, blind, and naked—

I counsel you to buy from Me gold refined in the fire, that you may be rich; and white garments, that you may be clothed, that the shame of your nakedness may not be revealed; and anoint your eyes with eye salve, that you may see.

As many as I love, I rebuke and chasten. Therefore be zealous and repent."

Revelation 3:14-19

Laodicea was a city far away from its water source, and water had to be brought to the city by a series of canals or ducts. By the time the water came out of the springs and traveled through these canals to the city, it was lukewarm. It was good for irrigation but terrible to drink.

God used this as an example of their spiritual condition. It was as if He said, "You're just like your water—terrible to drink." In fact, He said they were so lukewarm that He was going to spew them out of His mouth (Revelation 3:16). This was the problem: they weren't in the world, cold to God, rebelling against Him; but when they came to church, it was just a form and a function to them. They would go through praise and worship thinking about lunch. They could listen to the teaching of the Word, all the while wondering when it would end. They would hear scriptures on giving, but were more interested in giving to themselves than to the work of God. They did not have that drive for excellence—they were just lukewarm. God would rather have had them in the world being cold, negative sinners than to have them be lukewarm Christians.

Lukewarmness is like a deadly disease that comes upon Christians when they think they've "done enough." They feel their church is big enough and doing enough. They think there is no need to keep fighting—let the other people worry about the rest of the world. So instead of increasing, they maintain. A maintenance ministry is never doing the will of God. God is always on the increase.

Being lukewarm is closely associated with compromise. Compromise is accepting what we don't believe because we refuse to fight for what we do believe! What we compromise to gain, we will always lose. It happens in every Christian's life. We might think we don't want to offend the people in the office by letting them know we are born again, filled with the Holy Ghost believers. Rather than turning somebody off, we stay "low key" and laid back—we are acting like undercover agents. When people find out we're Christians and know that we haven't told anyone, they will know we are ashamed of our beliefs. We will lose the admiration and honor of the others which was what we were trying to gain in the first place.

We have been called by God to fight for excellence. Here are six areas to think about when asking yourself the question, "How excellent am I?"

Number one: How excellent am I in living a holy lifestyle? Am I an excellent example of holiness in all that I do and say, and in every area of my life?

Number two: How excellent am I in witnessing? Do I talk to the lost, bring people to church and help them to know the Lord?

Number three: Do I pray and listen to the voice of the Spirit who lives within me? Am I really following the Spirit, or do I basically do my own thing and ask God to bless it? How excellent am I in my walk with the Holy Spirit?

Number four: Am I fighting to prosper so I might be a blessing? Or do I accept just having enough money to meet my own needs and let the rest of the world be in need? How excellent am I in prosperity?

Number five: Do I really fight to help others, to serve in my church, to give of my time? Am I excellent in my service to others?

Number six: Am I building godly Christian relationships? Am I getting close to people? Am I confessing my faults with others? Am I letting them know me and getting to know them? Do I know people that I can trust and count on, who can trust and count on me? Proverbs says that if a man is to have friends, he must first show himself friendly (Proverbs 18:24). How excellent am I in my relationships?

When we fight for excellence, we put ourselves in a place where God will promote us. God will elevate us to that place of leadership and success where we can influence our companies, families, cities, states, and our world. We will never accomplish anything if we are content to be mediocre Christians who are "hanging in there until Jesus comes." But as people with a spirit of excellence, we will make a difference in our world.

4

Daniel: A Man
of Excellence

In the book of Daniel, chapter 5, we find
that Belshazzar, one of the kings of Babylon,
had a problem. He was greatly troubled and
confused by a vision he had seen of a man's
hand writing words on a wall. The queen
told him that Daniel, who had been made
master of the wise men by the king's own
father years earlier, could tell him the
meaning of the vision. Daniel was highly
thought of because of his reputation:

> **"Inasmuch as an excellent spirit,
> knowledge, understanding, inter-
> preting dreams, solving riddles, and
> explaining enigmas were found in this
> Daniel, whom the king named
> Belteshazzar, now let Daniel be called,
> and he will give the interpretation."**
>
> **Daniel 5:12**

I pray for myself and for all of our staff at Christian Faith Center—that we will have this same spirit: one of excellence, knowledge, understanding, having the ability to interpret dreams, answer hard questions, solve hard problems, and dissolve doubts.

Daniel had an excellent spirit. The spirit of his mind, the spirit of his life, his countenance, his manner of living—all were excellent. What exactly does this mean? Let's look at Daniel's life and see what this spirit is and how he developed it.

Daniel was a Hebrew, a Jewish boy, who had been captured by King Nebuchadnezzar of Babylon. Along with all of the other young, healthy, bright, strong men of Israel, he was taken to Babylon.

Babylon was a great city. It was the epitome of everything imaginable in the then-known world. It's architecture was greater than that of any other city. The 'hanging gardens' of Babylon are still known as a wonder of the world. The streets were lined with columns and pillars. The walls of the buildings which lined the streets of Babylon were covered with paintings and great mosaics. It also had a great university.

It had more knowledge, more of the world's wisdom, than any other city known at that time. Under Nebuchadnezzar's reign, Babylon had wealth and conquered every other great society throughout the world.

Now imagine Daniel! He was a young man somewhere between 18 and 25 years of age going into the greatest city in the world! The king's plan was to feed his young Hebrew captives the best food, the best wine and give them the best education because he was going to build the strongest, wisest and sharpest young men possible to lead his nation.

Now notice what Daniel did after entering Babylon: **"But Daniel purposed in his heart that he would not defile himself with the portion of the king's delicacies, nor with the wine which he drank; therefore he requested of the chief of the eunuchs that he might not defile himself"** (Daniel 1:8).

It was obvious that Babylon was a greater society than Israel. It would have been very easy for Daniel to say, "These guys are definitely smarter than we are. They have more wisdom, strength and money. Their gods must be better than our

God." But Daniel purposed in his heart not to defile himself with their lifestyle.

I believe the first key to having an excellent spirit is to have purpose in your heart. Have you ever looked at a person and thought, "That person has real heart?" What you mean is that they have something in them—intestinal fortitude—"guts," if you please—drive, desire, and motivation. They overcome obstacles and don't go along with peer pressure. They are not easily swayed. There is something within them that makes them a unique individual. They stand out in the crowd. They are not afraid to be different. They are not afraid to fight. And even when they get knocked down, they have the "guts" to get up again.

Daniel was an individual who had "heart." Daniel purposed in his heart to go against the greatest society in the world. He would not become a part of it. That took heart!

Daniel didn't come from a nation that had trained him to be a spiritual giant. The land of Israel was filled with people of compromise. That is why they were easily overthrown. If they had been serving God, they would have defeated Nebuchadnezzar.

In spite of his living in a nation of compromise and mediocrity, Daniel decided to discipline himself and not become caught up in the spirit of that city. Daniel wouldn't even eat the food that was there. He decided to be different...to stand out. It took major determination on his part to stand against the system of Babylon in which he found himself.

Secondly, Daniel developed an excellent spirit by refusing to be defiled by the world. Daniel was not going to accept Babylon's way of doing things. He was not going to go along with what was socially acceptable. He refused to be defiled. The word "defile" simply means "made unclean." In a more literal sense, it means to be destroyed. Daniel refused to be influenced and affected by the world. Though there were many temptations to compromise, he kept himself strong in his lifestyle with God.

Thirdly, Daniel developed an excellent spirit by disciplining himself. I'm convinced that if we cannot discipline ourselves, we will never have an excellent spirit. Discipline should affect every area of our life: the physical, mental, spiritual, and financial areas. Every area of our life should be disciplined if we are going to have an excellent spirit.

The fourth way Daniel developed an excellent spirit was by loving his enemies. **"Now God had brought Daniel into the favor and good will of the chief of the eunuchs" (Daniel 1:9).** The 'chief of the eunuchs' was the man that the king put in charge of these young Israelites. He was responsible to make sure they ate the right foods, exercised properly and were taught well.

If Daniel had shown a rebellious attitude toward the chief eunuch and had allowed bitter hatred to come between them, things surely would have been different. But that's not the approach that Daniel took. He opened himself to love this man and to build a relationship with him. Because of this, God was able to work through the love between Daniel and his captor.

An excellent spirit doesn't stand up with righteous indignation and a judgmental attitude. An excellent spirit builds relationships with tender love, even with the enemy.

Let's look at the fifth aspect of Daniel's excellent spirit. When King Nebuchadnezzar had a troubling dream one night, he was very upset. He woke up nervous and in a

cold sweat (Daniel 2:1). In Nebuchadnezzar's day and age, dreams always meant
something. They were considered very
important. In the morning, however, he
couldn't remember what his dream was
about.

The king called in his magicians,
astronomers, and wise counselors and
commanded them to not only interpret the
dream, but to also tell him what the dream
was! Of course there was no way these men
could possibly do that. They let the king
know that his request was totally
unreasonable. No one could do what the
king had asked of them.

King Nebuchadnezzar was very
displeased with these men and told them
that if they didn't do what he had requested,
they would lose their heads! The magicians
and counselors could not perform, so a
decree was issued to have them *all* killed.
Since Daniel was one of the "wise men," he
was also under this sentence of death.

Daniel's response to the situation is
found in Daniel 2:14: **"Then with counsel
and wisdom Daniel answered Arioch, the
captain of the king's guard, who had gone
out to kill the wise men of Babylon."** Daniel

answered with counsel and wisdom. He was developing an excellent spirit by controlling his tongue. He could have talked like the rest of the wise men. But instead, Daniel answered with wisdom and counsel. He controlled his tongue and spoke with wisdom.

> "He answered and said to Arioch the king's captain, 'Why is the decree from the king so urgent?' Then Arioch made the decision known to Daniel.
>
> So Daniel went in and asked the king to give him time, that he might tell the king the interpretation.
>
> Then Daniel went to his house, and made the decision known to Hananiah, Mishael, and Azariah, his companions,
>
> That they might seek mercies from the God of heaven concerning this secret, so that Daniel and his companions might not perish with the rest of the wise men of Babylon.
>
> Then the secret was revealed to Daniel in a night vision. So Daniel blessed the God of heaven."
>
> **Daniel 2:15-19**

Here is the sixth step in developing an excellent spirit: Walk by faith. Daniel didn't have any idea what the dream was or what would be the interpretation. Daniel had no word from God that he would even find out, but he went to the king and asked for more time so that he could come back with the interpretation.

I believe Daniel was simply walking by faith and trusting that God would bring him the answer when he went before the king again. Faith believes God will work. Daniel walked by faith.

The seventh way Daniel developed an excellent spirit was through prayer. **"...that they might seek mercies from the God of heaven concerning this secret..." (Daniel 2:18).** Daniel and his companions prayed for mercy. They sought God and said, "Lord, give us the answer! Help us in this circumstance."

We find throughout the book of Daniel that he was a man of prayer. When Daniel was told he couldn't pray, he opened up his window and prayed all day long. He knew where his source and his help were found. We will never have an excellent spirit if we don't have a lifestyle of prayer.

The eighth way Daniel developed an excellent spirit was by having close companions. When he discovered why the decree was issued for their deaths, he made it known to his three companions. Their Babylonian names were Hananiah, Mishael, and Azariah, but we all know them as Shadrach, Meschach, and Abednego.

Notice that Daniel didn't have to "call the prayer chain." He just went to his friends. He didn't have to call the pastor; he just went to his friends. The Christian life is a life of relationships. We all need to have people who are close to us so that when a need arises we can call on them and say, "Here's the situation. Let's get in agreement."

We need companions and partners. What does fellowship mean? It means "having more than one fellow in the ship." We are not alone. A house divided is not God's way. An excellent spirit is developed through relationships with other people. We need to have people around us who have the same spirit so that we can grow in excellence together.

The ninth way to develop an excellent spirit is by remembering that God is our source. Through God's help, Daniel was able to tell the king his dream.

"Daniel answered in the presence of the king, and said, 'The secret which

the king has demanded, the wise men, the astrologers, the magicians, and the soothsayers cannot declare to the king.

But there is a God in heaven who reveals secrets, and He has made known to King Nebuchadnezzar what will be in the latter days. Your dream, and the visions of your head upon your bed, were these:"

Daniel 2:27-28

Daniel told the king that no man could answer his questions or interpret his dream. What the king asked could not be done in the natural, but only through God in heaven. What is an excellent spirit? Giving all glory to God. We will have an excellent spirit when we remember God is our source.

Lastly, Daniel was consistent. Time after time, in every circumstance Daniel faced including the den of lions, he remained consistent in his attitude toward life, his way of dealing with people, and his relationship with God. Daniel had an excellent spirit because he was consistent.

5
Wisdom and Strategy Bring Success

When I think of someone with an excellent spirit, I think of someone who has wisdom.

Wisdom always begins with knowledge then progresses to understanding, and eventually becomes wisdom. Knowledge is data or facts. Understanding is the ability to use this information and know what it means. Wisdom is the application of those facts—being able to put them into practice and make them work.

In order to live an excellent life, to have excellence in everything we do, we need to have wisdom. To be successful parents, have fulfilling careers, and continue to grow in our own personal Christian walk requires the use of wisdom. If we try to stumble our way through life, we will end up in a mess. We must be wise with our time, our words, and our commitments. It takes wisdom to handle all of the responsibilities of life in an excellent way.

If we were to ask the average person in church what his strategy or plan was for handling his job and family, he wouldn't be able to tell us. The average person has never come to a point of really applying wisdom to managing his life, his family, his schedule and his career. He just tries his best to keep it all together. Wisdom will create the strategy or plan for getting the job done well.

We can have the drive and the desire to do something, but without wisdom, we could spend our time doing things that won't produce the best results! Wisdom— God's wisdom—will always provide a strategy that will produce big results. Along with wisdom there always comes a strategy or a plan. Remember that wisdom is the application of knowledge!

Many times we have the concept that being led of the Spirit means not knowing what we are going to do until after we do it. I don't believe that's the way God operates. I believe God gives us wisdom. And from that wisdom we develop a strategy from which our success and victory come. We will accomplish our goals, fulfill our tasks and get the job done! We will raise our kids properly, have a happy marriage, prosper financially, keep our checkbooks balanced, and manage to have money in our savings accounts! We all want to shout and feel the glory of victory. But victory doesn't come unless we have the right strategy. And the strategy won't come unless we have the wisdom.

When Solomon became the king after David died, he sought after wisdom:

"On that night God appeared to Solomon, and said to him, 'Ask! What shall I give you?'

And Solomon said to God: 'You have shown great mercy to David my father, and have made me king in his place.

Now, O LORD God, let Your promise to David my father be established, for You have made me king over a people like the dust of the earth in multitude.

Now give me wisdom and knowledge, that I may go out and come in before this people; for who can judge this great people of Yours?'

And God said to Solomon: 'Because this was in your heart, and you have not asked riches or wealth or honor or the life of your enemies, nor have you asked long life—but have asked wisdom and knowledge for yourself, that you may judge My people over whom I have made you king—

Wisdom and knowledge are granted to you; and I will give you riches and wealth and honor, such as none of the kings have had who have been before you, nor shall any after you have the like.'"

II Chronicles 1:7-12

Solomon obviously was a wise man even before he asked God for wisdom because he was astute enough to ask for that instead of riches, wealth or honor. But through wisdom, Solomon was able to obtain all those other things as well. How did that happen? When we have wisdom, we will know the strategy for being successful, which leads to riches, wealth and honor. Solomon got it all because he had wisdom.

Sometimes Christian leaders are very foolish. To say that we don't care about strategies, details, and plans, shows our lack of wisdom. As leaders, we should have wisdom and bring forth the strategies needed to succeed. Other people can put these plans into action and make them happen—then we all enjoy the success.

At one of Dr. Ed Cole's meetings, a man asked him, "Would you agree with me that my wife will come home? She doesn't love me. She left me and my marriage is falling apart, but I want to bring it back together." So Dr. Cole prayed for him and then asked the man what he was going to do to get his wife back.

The man replied, "I'm just going to rejoice in the Lord, forgive her and love her and believe she is coming back."

Dr. Cole said, "No, let me ask you one more time. What are you going to **DO** to bring your wife back home?"

He replied, "I'm just going to praise the Lord and believe God. I forgive her and love her, and I know God will work it all out."

Dr. Cole had a beautiful response for this man. He said, "When you have lost your first love, it's because you stopped doing your first works. And until you get back to doing your first works, you will never get back your first love."

What is the strategy going to be? If you don't have a strategy, you will never have success. Do the first works and you will recapture the first love. How did you get that love the first time? Go and do those same things again.

Solomon received wisdom from God: **"And God gave Solomon wisdom and exceedingly great understanding, and largeness of heart like the sand on the seashore. Thus Solomon's wisdom excelled the wisdom of all the men of the East and all the wisdom of Egypt" (I Kings 4:29-30).**

Solomon's wisdom excelled the wisdom of all the world. God gave him much more than anyone had ever had before. He was wiser than all men.

> **"Wisdom is the principal thing; therefore get wisdom. And in all your getting, get understanding."**
>
> **Exalt her, and she will promote you; she will bring you honor, when you embrace her."**
>
> **Proverbs 4:7-8**
>
> **"Happy is the man who finds wisdom, and the man who gains understanding;**

For her proceeds are better than the profits of silver, and her gain than fine gold.

Proverbs 3:13-14

Why is wisdom better than silver and fine gold? Because if you have wisdom, you can get all the silver and fine gold you will ever need. But without wisdom, no matter how much money you get, you will never be happy.

Wisdom is characterized as a tree of life that brings pleasantness and peace (Proverbs 3:17-18). Isn't it interesting that wisdom will bring everything you will ever need in life? Wisdom will provide happiness, long life, pleasantness, peace, and every good thing. The fool is always lacking. The wise man and woman have everything they need.

How do we get wisdom? There are several ways.

First of all, we can ask God for wisdom. We will be unstable if we lack wisdom. But we will continue to be unstable if we pray for wisdom and then doubt whether we are going to receive it or not. When we pray for wisdom, we must pray in faith believing that we receive.

"If any of you lacks wisdom, let him ask of God, who gives to all liberally and without reproach, and it will be given to him.

But let him ask in faith, with no doubting, for he who doubts is like a wave of the sea driven and tossed by the wind.

For let not that man suppose that he will receive anything from the Lord;

He is a double-minded man, unstable in all his ways."

James 1:5-8

Secondly, study for wisdom. "Be diligent to present yourself approved to God, a worker who does not need to be ashamed, rightly dividing the word of truth" (II Timothy 2:15). Why do we listen to teaching tapes about leadership, management and the Word? Because we want wisdom. Why do we invest money into study materials? Because we want wisdom. Spending money on teaching tools should not be an option. If we want to increase in wisdom, we need to study. If we don't get study materials to increase our wisdom, then our ministries and our lives will not increase. Studying brings growth in the Lord. We do not want to miss out on God's will for our lives.

The third way to get wisdom is to fellowship with those who are wise. **"He who walks with wise men will be wise, but the companion of fools will be destroyed"** (Proverbs 13:20). We need to fellowship with wise men and women. It's good to minister to people and lift them up. But we must guard ourselves because very often we give the excuse of getting together to minister to people, when in reality we like to be with those people because we are comfortable around them.

When you find yourself able to just "shoot the breeze" and not feel challenged, then you had better examine yourself to make sure you are not a companion of fools. When you get together with someone to minister to them, do it to give *your* spirit to them, not to receive *their* spirit. When you are fellowshipping with your neighbors, your church family or your relatives, you need to know what "spirit" they are giving you. If they are not giving you a spirit of excellence, then you need to make some drastic changes.

Guard yourself and seek fellowship for wisdom. Get around excellent people like those described in the book of Proverbs. Walk with the wise and you will be wise also.

The fourth way to acquire wisdom is to practice wisdom. When we make decisions, we need to ask ourselves, "What would be the wisest thing to do right now?" Some of us have been fools for so long that doing wise things feels very strange to us. It feels funny and we don't really like it. As we practice using wisdom, we will overcome those feelings.

We must pray for wisdom, study for wisdom, fellowship with wisdom, and practice wisdom!

Successful Strategies

As we have already briefly discussed, once we have wisdom, we then need a strategy. Strategy is the science of planning and directing and the skill of managing and planning. It is an artful means to an end.

Some of us can make it to the end, but did we do it artfully? We got the kids up, fed, cleaned, dressed, and in the car. But did we do it artfully? The answer to this question indicates whether or not we had a strategy.

Strategy is an artful means to an end. It is the step-by-step process by which we accomplish our goals. Many times we accomplish our goals, but we do it in a hit-or-miss manner. We try one way and it doesn't work. So we try something else and it works a little better, and eventually we get the job done.

I had a friend in high school who would always tell us he was going to be a millionaire. When we asked him how he was going to do it, he would simply tell us to wait and see. This guy ran around saying he was going to be a millionaire! Of course, he ended up going to jail with the rest of us. I haven't heard from him for quite a while, so I doubt that he has accomplished his financial goal.

Strategy is what determines whether or not you reach your goals. Strategy makes all the difference. Anyone can say, "I have a dream." But how are you going to accomplish it? What is your strategy to achieve that dream?

Here are some steps you can use in developing strategies. We could also say these are processes of establishing and reaching goals.

Before we can set strategies, we must know our role. We must know our own gifts, talents and callings.

Robert Schuller has a saying: "Your role, plus your goal, plus the toll equals success."

This means you have to know your role before you can establish an appropriate goal. Then you have to be willing to pay the toll. It's going to cost you something—are you willing to pay it? Only then will you have success.

The whole process begins with knowing your role. Where do you fit into the whole scheme of things? What are your gifts and talents? Knowing yourself is very important in establishing strategies for your life. What are you really called to do? If you are trying to do something you are not called to do, you will be very frustrated. Even if you accomplish the goal, you won't be fulfilled by it. Take the time to know your role, your gifts, and your talents.

The second step is to decide where you want to be at a particular time. What is your destination? Where do you want your life to be at a certain time? You need to set certain time frames for accomplishing your goals or they will become meaningless. Decide where you want your department, your project, your life to be at a specific time. Don't just pick arbitrary targets or decide on some number that sounds good to you. Be realistic and practical. If you set realistic goals, then you will set yourself up to succeed and not fail. Be optimistic and don't feel bad when you fall short of your goals. I would rather shoot a little high and miss than aim low and hit the mark. Just keep pressing onward!

The third step in developing successful strategies is to realize what it will take to accomplish your goals. This is where you really become a strategist.

Jesus said, **"For which of you, intending to build a tower, does not sit down first and count the cost, whether he has enough to finish it—lest after he has laid the foundation, and is not able to finish it, all who see it begin to mock him..." (Luke 14:28-29).** All of us have failed at different times in reaching our goals because we did not understand exactly what was involved in accomplishing those goals.

Some people we knew years ago had lived for twelve years in an unfinished house. The interior walls were two-by-fours without insulation or sheetrock. The kids had a door going in every direction because their bedroom walls were only framed in. The wife piled their dishes where the cupboards were going to be someday. They lived like that for twelve years! All that beheld their house mocked that husband.

Jesus told us to count the cost before we start anything. That simply means we need to understand what steps we must take to reach the goal. We may need to gather people who can help us with those steps and help us understand more clearly what needs to be done. We may not understand how to reach our goals, but that doesn't mean we have an excuse to give up on them.

Have you ever told someone that you would help them with a project before you understood exactly what was involved? Then when they told you about all the things that needed to be done, you realized you really didn't have the time to help them after all. Now you are considered irresponsible because you went back on your word. If your word is no good, your character is no good. When people begin to question your character, they can no longer trust your leadership.

If a pastor announces to his church, "We're going to build a 10,000-seat sanctuary by next year," without realizing that it will cost $15,000,000, require 40 acres of land, and will over-challenge the congregation, he will have to come back later and say, "Oops, I was only kidding." In the minds of the people his word is no longer good. They wonder about his character. If something like this happens several times, they will question his character and his leadership.

The fourth step is to ask yourself the question, "Am I willing to pay the price?" Your goal may be to have 25 home meetings, but are you willing to spend the time it takes to shepherd all those meetings? Are you willing to deal with the problems that will arise with having new leaders and groups? Are you willing to pay the price?

"Bless God, I want a 5,000-square-foot home!" Do you know how long it takes to clean a home that big? Do you know what it will cost to heat a home of that size? Have you considered all the steps involved in accomplishing that goal? You may come to the conclusion that you honestly don't want to reach that goal.

We are always talking about growth at Christian Faith Center. We talk about having 10,000 or 20,000 people attending! One day I really started thinking about what having a church that size would mean and asked myself, "Do I really want that? My life is great right now. I work hard, have plenty of opportunities to preach and live well. All the needs at the church are met and we have a beautiful, gifted staff. Everything is great just the way it is."

"Do I really want to pastor 10,000 or 20,000 people? It would be more of a sacrifice than anything. My life couldn't get much better than it is right now. In fact, I would just end up with more work, more challenges, and more situations to deal with."

"Do I really want a new building? Our current facilities are pretty good. We could do a few things to enhance them a little but no major improvements are needed."

"Do we really need to expand our school? Why not let it stay the size it is now and just tell the students on the waiting list that there is no more room?"

"Why hassle with growth? We are all having fun serving God and giving everything we have into the ministry."

Do you know the real reason most churches don't grow? The pastor doesn't want it to! When he begins to look at the steps involved with growth such as hiring, training, and firing staff along with everything else involved, it's just easier to stay small to avoid all that hassle.

When you start considering the steps involved with accomplishing your goal, you may change your goal.

The fifth step in developing a strategy is to establish a daily discipline. If you are not willing to do something today to work toward your goal, that goal is really just a fantasy.

You could decide you want to lose twelve pounds by next year, but if you aren't willing to work on that goal today, you probably won't lose any weight at all. The procrastination of working on your goals "now," is a sure sign your goals are not really a part of you. They will never come to pass, because the faith you need to accomplish them is always "now" (Hebrews 11:1).

Remember, the goal must be a part of your heart. If it's not a part of your heart, you won't have the motivation to do something *every day* to reach it. If it's not a part of your heart, you will rationalize and procrastinate your daily discipline. When it is a part of you, you will have the energy and desire to be disciplined.

You also need to visualize and verbalize your goal. In order to make your goal a part of you, you should think and talk about it often. This is a valuable and important part of your strategy. The focus now is to make this goal real to yourself.

The sixth step in setting your strategy is to know the facts and make any necessary adjustments. The Living Bible says, **"Any enterprise is built by wise planning, becomes strong through common sense, and profits wonderfully by keeping abreast of the facts" (Proverbs 24:3-4, TLB).**

What are the facts? Let's say your goal is to have 300 kids in children's church by the end of the year. How many did you have this week? You may guess about 270 kids (the room was jammed!), when if you had actually counted, you would have discovered there were only 112 kids in the room. It is easy to deceive yourself. It's easy to think that you have prayed for an hour when you have only prayed for thirty minutes. It's easy to think that you have really worked out, when an exercise expert could tell you that you are not even getting your heart rate to the minimum requirement.

When you stay abreast of the facts, you will realize your need to make adjustments. If you don't reach your goal in the time you had established, just make an adjustment. Don't say, "Oh, Lord. What did I do wrong? Oh no, I didn't make it." Make an adjustment and keep on going toward your goal by carrying out your strategy.

Don't be afraid to adjust your course. That is part of life. Be quick to revise your strategy and don't just stick with something that's not working.

The seventh and final step is: Don't quit! Keep going! It's all right if you didn't reach the goal exactly like you thought you would. Keep going! Don't quit!

6

Attitudes That Produce Results

A great part of leadership success is based on our attitudes. *Attitude* simply means *our way of thinking, the way we view things, the way we handle things mentally*. Our leadership attitudes have a great deal to do with what we produce in leadership.

Too often we feel we don't have what it takes to be great leaders. However, the truth is we don't lack leadership ability; we just need to *believe* that we have what it takes to be effective leaders. Our thinking is usually the difference between "can" and "cannot." We must have an attitude that says, "I can!"

Most of the time, your attitude determines your success or failure. As a leader, if you have the right attitude about what you are doing, you will produce good things. It's generally not a matter of going back to school, reading more books, getting more finances or anything else. The crucial factor is having the right leadership attitudes. This coupled with whatever talents and abilities you already have will be more than enough for you to be an effective leader.

Getting Results

As a leader thinks, so is he (or she). Your way of thinking or your attitude controls the results and fruit of your ministry and life.

Our goal should be to do those things which produce the results that we desire and that God desires. This may not sound spiritual, but getting results is the name of the game. Someone once said, "Winning isn't everything, it's *the only thing*." This attitude is vital to having a successful ministry.

Being successful as a church is not everything, it is *the only thing*. We must have no other options. We <u>will</u> grow; we <u>will</u> save sinners; we <u>will</u> raise up happy, prosperous, successful Christian people. We can't accept anything less. Maintaining our present status is not even a consideration. "Hanging in there" is not part of the plan. Results are the focus. Making a difference in the lives of people, seeing growth, progress, healing, salvation, prosperity and holiness are the only results with which we will be satisfied.

If you don't have this kind of attitude but you are around people who do, you will be extremely frustrated with the continual push for results. Or possibly *you* are the one pushing for results and everyone around you wants to maintain. These people must either change their attitude to match yours or they will leave.

Jesus said, **"Either make the tree good and its fruit good, or else make the tree bad and its fruit bad; for a tree is known by its fruit"** (Matthew 12:33). "Fruit" is just another way of saying "results." The Bible is telling us to either get in and produce results for the kingdom of God, or get out and be corrupt. Do one or the other. Don't sit around the church in maintenance mode playing religious games. I'm interested in seeing fruit. I'm not interested in intentions or what we hope or plan to do.

Every church and church member should desire to do good things. But wanting good things and actually seeing them happen are two different things. *Intentions*

don't count—fruit does. There is a saying that goes—"The way to hell is paved with good intentions." What we're interested in is doing whatever it takes to produce *results*. What does it matter if we talk about wanting to be great ministers, teachers or servants? What matters is the fruit or *results* we are producing.

When it comes to results, guard against the urgent things that divert you away from the important things. We can get caught up in *little* tasks all day, everyday. We spend so much time on our minor emergencies that we never get around to the important things that will really make a difference. Don't let *the urgent* control you any longer.

Words are powerful! Here are two words that are extremely important when it comes to producing results: *pragmatic and concise*.

Pragmatic means concern with the actual practice, not the theory or speculation. How much do you think is theory and how much do you think is actuality? How much time do you spend on the speculation of things that really don't produce results? How much time do you spend on things that really work?

There's a theory that the average business spends 80 percent of it's time on unimportant, urgent things, and the remaining 20 percent on important, pragmatic things. It would be great if we could turn that statistic around. We deceive ourselves by not being pragmatic people and not focusing on what is really needed.

The other word to put in our minds is *concise*. *Concise means the cutting away of all superfluous data.* It is getting down to the real issues, getting down to the nitty-gritty. Some of us need to talk more concisely. So much time is wasted by simply "beating around the bush." It takes so long to get to the point, if we ever do get there at all!

Remember, the <u>urgent</u> *is usually not* <u>important</u>. For myself, the important things are: prayer, studying to feed the flock of God, knowing the mind of the Spirit for our congregation, my relationships with the staff and the leaders in our church, the training and leading of leaders and home meetings.

Let's not be people who spend our lives dealing with unimportant issues that waste our time. Our attitude should be one of excellence and one of producing results.

Give yourself to those things that produce fruit. *Be pragmatic and concise in all you do.* Then the results will be great.

Excellence or Excuses

As I've mentioned in previous chapters, having an excellent spirit is an attitude of the heart. It is not something that we do just from our minds. Living an excellent life means being excellent in every area of our life, and that can only be accomplished through a decision of the heart not a decision of the mind!

Many times we make decisions because we know we *should*. But we can't live on what we *should* do, so after a while we're back to where we were before we started. If Daniel had only been motivated by what he thought he *should* do, he would have done what he really wanted to do as soon as he got away from his parents, the peer pressure, society, and his own culture. But Daniel had purposed in his heart to have an excellent spirit, and that maintained him through all circumstances.

I don't believe we can decide to be excellent in one area and mediocre in another. It's our lifestyle—something that is built into our hearts—that affects every area of our lives. It becomes part of everything we are and everything we do. We rise no higher than our personal commitment, so we must have a commitment to excellence.

Frustration comes when we try to become excellent at certain things instead of having an excellent spirit. The Bible doesn't say Daniel was excellent at counseling, excellent in interpreting dreams, excellent at keeping his body fit, and excellent at praying. The Bible says *Daniel had an excellent spirit*, which means that everything he did was done in an excellent manner.

We shouldn't try to become excellent secretaries, counselors, teachers, or pastors. We should become excellent people. Then out of our excellent spirits will come excellent things. We will wear ourselves out *trying to do <u>things</u> in an excellent manner*. But if we develop an excellent spirit, then everything we do will be a reflection of what is on the "inside."

In our commitment to excellence, we have to guard against rationalization and excuses because these will create mediocrity and negate excellence. We rationalize by comparing ourselves with others. It's easy to feel like we are doing well when we compare ourselves to a particular group. For instance, if I compared what our church is doing to all the other churches within a five-mile radius, I could really "praise the Lord." In comparison to the rest of the group, all is well and we are doing great! However, if I start comparing our church to other churches around the world, then I may reach an entirely different conclusion. I could end up with many discouraging thoughts about our ministry. Comparisons are very often a way of feeding our excuses. But you can't live on comparisons. Paul said it is unwise to compare ourselves among ourselves (II Corinthians 10:12).

Many times when we are not thinking excellently, we view excellence as a negative thing. We may say things like, "Those people are always concerned with how they look. They are only satisfied if they are above everyone else." That is the rationalization about excellence by the mediocre person. It may be true that some people seek excellence only for their own ego, to make themselves feel important, and to be above someone else. But that's no excuse for us to accept our mediocrity. We must guard against this type of attitude.

We often look for loopholes to make our lack of excellence "okay." If a pastor is preaching against overweight and lack of physical discipline, we might think, "He is so fleshly minded. All he talks about is the body and being skinny. God doesn't really care about that stuff. Everyone knows bodily exercise profiteth little."

That may sound nice, but it's a nice, spiritual-sounding excuse to stay fat. In reality, we had better go after all the "little profits" we can get. If we want to live long on the earth, we had better take care of our physical "temple" because God will destroy those who defile it (I Corinthians 3:17).

Time is another one of those areas we can always use as an excuse. Lack of time becomes a beautiful excuse for lack of prayer, study, exercise, or time with family and friends. The truth is, we always have time to do what we really want to do.

God is seeking for attitudes of excellence and He desires that we have a commitment to excellence. When I think of Jesus and the way He walked, the way He lived, the way He carried Himself, I know He did everything excellently. I believe that Jesus spoke excellently, cared excellently, dressed excellently, and carried Himself with an excellent spirit. He is our example. Jesus said that the things He did, we would do also (John 14:12). We just need to follow Him.

I believe that in order to do what Jesus did, we must start by having the desire. We can't operate from what we think we should do or what someone else is doing. If these are our motives, we will fail! When we have real heartfelt desires, God will give us the desires of our hearts.

Also needed is motivation or drive. Perhaps you feel like you really want something, but you just don't know if you can ever achieve that desire. If you have the drive, that question will never come up. You will always have the energy to make it.

Drive can be developed by having a strong enough desire. And desire is developed by feeding it. You always desire what you feed on. Smokers didn't desire cigarettes until they started feeding them into their mouths. Then they desired them. Drinkers didn't desire alcohol until they started consuming it. Once they started, they began to desire it.

We don't crave certain things until we become involved with them. And once we do, our desire for these things grows more and more. So we can feed our desires and make them strong.

Agreement: The Place of Power

"Again I say to you that if two of you agree on earth concerning anything that they ask, it will be done for them by My Father in heaven.

For where two or three are gathered together in My name, I am there in the midst of them."

Matthew 18:19-20

Jesus tells us that agreement is a place of power. It is what brings results and allows God's Spirit to work in our lives.

These same verses in the Amplified Bible read:

"Again I tell you, if two of you on earth agree (harmonize together, make a symphony together) about whatever [anything and everything] they may ask, it will come to pass and be done for them by My Father in heaven.

For wherever two or three are gathered (drawn together as My followers) in (into) My name, there I AM in the midst of them."

Matthew 18:19-20 (Amplified)

When the scripture says we are gathered together in His name, we could also say we are gathered together *in agreement*. In other words, if we are gathered together in disagreement, God isn't going to show up there and He won't answer prayer.

Agreement is a place of power. It is not just an outward sign. Agreement is a spirit, an attitude. It goes deeper than any outward expression. I've seen people in church who are falling asleep but who are in agreement with me. I've seen other people who look like they are listening intently but actually are in disagreement with me. Agreement is not necessarily an outward expression, although it can be. Agreement is a spirit, an attitude, and an inward conviction.

In marriage we must have agreement and harmony even though there may be many things we disagree on. Married couples may disagree on a number of things, but if the husband and wife share a harmony in their hearts, then everything will work. However, if disagreement hits their hearts there will be big trouble.

My wife and I may debate about the color of towels for the bathroom, the schedule for this week, where we are going to eat dinner, what kind of clothes we are going to wear, and how we discipline the kids. We may disagree, debate and thoroughly discuss these items back and forth. But as long as we have harmony in our hearts with each other, everything will be all right. We will still be married years from now.

If that disagreement hits the heart, however, we would hear things like, "I don't know why we are married anyway. Maybe I don't love you anymore." I have counselled married couples who are having problems and that is their normal way of talking. Disagreement has entered their hearts and now they are experiencing problems.

I feel the same way about our church staff relationships. A staff member can challenge anything he wants to challenge. He can confront anyone else in staff meetings. He can disagree with anything just as long as there is harmony in his heart. However, as soon as the harmony is gone and is replaced by disagreement, there is trouble.

An independent spirit is a wicked thing. This attitude will eventually destroy relationships and cause people to go their own way. Jesus said, **"Every kingdom divided against itself is brought to desolation, and every city or house divided against itself will not stand" (Matthew 12:25).** A person with an independent spirit says, "I don't need anyone, and I don't have to agree with anyone. I'm going to do it my way, one way or another." That spirit separates them from everyone else and will cause them to fall.

Agreement is a place of power and disagreement is the way to destruction. Many times an independent spirit is disguised with words such as "vision" or "motivation," or "the rest of you are too slow," or "you don't care about what I want to do." But all of these attitudes are manifestations of an independent spirit.

When we're in agreement with someone, we must do whatever is necessary to stay in agreement with them. We should not be afraid to voice our disagreement but we must keep harmony in our hearts. We are not trying to find points we disagree on, but instead find places where we agree. That's how we stay in a place of power. That's where we have real authority, strength, friendships and relationships. It's okay to disagree but we must keep that spirit of harmony in our hearts.

Turning Stress Into Success

I turn stress into success. Stress is good! Stress is fun! Stress is what I look for, because I want more success.

Remember the old science fiction movies where the good guy would run into one of those monsters that lived on energy? Everything the monster ate just made it bigger. It would eat the power plants, the dam, and eventually the whole town. That's how I envision myself. I feed on stress. The worse it gets, the more motivated I become. The harder it is, the bigger I get! The more problems I face, the more strength rises up within me. Every leader has to have that kind of an attitude to stay on top of the pressures.

In the sport of cycling, when the cyclists have to climb the French Alps or Pyrennes Mountains (which average 10,000 and 12,000 feet), that's when the champion spirit comes alive. They start eating mountains for lunch! Those athletes get a flow of energy. The tougher it gets, the meaner they get.

We need to have the attitude or way of thinking that says, "When it's hard, I get better. When there's pressure, I get motivated. When there's stress, I get excited!" Unfortunately many of us get worried instead of excited. It's our attitude that makes the difference. The way we think makes the difference. We can decide to have a leadership attitude that says, "When the pressure is on, I love it!" We have to be able to thrive on stress if we want to be involved with succeeding, growing, changing ministries.

We find a good example of winning under stress in the conflict between David and Goliath. Israel was under attack from the Philistines. They sent out their champion, a giant named Goliath, to defy the armies of God:

> "Then he stood and cried out to the armies of Israel, and said to them, 'Why have you come out to line up for battle? Am I not a Philistine, and you the servants of Saul? Choose a man for yourselves, and let him come down to me.
>
> If he is able to fight with me and kill me, then we will be your servants. But if I prevail against him and kill him, then you shall be our servants and serve us.'
>
> And the Philistine said, 'I defy the armies of Israel this day; give me a man, that we may fight together.'

> **When Saul and all Israel heard these words of the Philistine, they were dismayed and greatly afraid."**
>
> **I Samuel 17:8-11**

The stress was on! How did the men of Israel react to the pressure of Goliath's challenge?

> **"And all the men of Israel, when they saw the man, fled from him and were dreadfully afraid."**
>
> **I Samuel 17:24**

Then David arrived on the scene. He was just a teenager at the time. He wasn't some great warrior, but his attitude was completely different from Saul's and the rest of the army.

> **"Then David said to Saul, 'Let no man's heart fail because of him; your servant will go and fight with this Philistine.'"**
>
> **I Samuel 17:32**

Isn't that amazing? The only difference between this seventeen-year-old boy and the rest of Israel was the way he thought. David didn't have any skill, any education, or any weapons that the rest of them didn't have. In fact, he had *less* than what they had—no armor and no sword. All he had was a way of thinking. David had a winning attitude and was willing to do something. He saw a giant and said, "There's lunch!" His greatest weapon was his attitude!

> **"Then David said to the Philistine, 'You come to me with a sword, with a spear, and with a javelin. But I come to you in the name of the LORD of hosts, the God of the armies of Israel, whom you have defied.**
>
> **This day the LORD will deliver you into my hand, and I will strike you and take your head from you. And this day I will give the carcasses of the camp of the Philistines to the birds of the air and the wild beasts of the earth, that all the earth may know that there is a God in Israel.'"**
>
> **I Samuel 17:45-46**

David was a bold teenager! But he knew God. He had a way of thinking that said, "This stress, this pressure, this giant, this problem will not stand against us! Let's go out there and take his head!"

You must have that same kind of spirit if you want to be a leader in the ministry. Pressure will come. There will be months when the finances aren't there. Are you going to crumble and wail about your poor budget? Or are you going to rise up and say, "I'm not controlled by that budget! I believe God."

There may be times when the world will talk badly about the church. They may think you are crazy and your church is a cult. That kind of talk can get you down and make you weak, scared and worried. People may not want anything more to do with you.

You have a decision to make! Will pressure be a motivation or will it be a burden? Is it fuel for your fire or will it put your fire out? You must develop a leadership attitude that says, "When things get tough, I get going. I get tough; I get stronger; I move forward."

Most millionaires are developed during times of great financial chaos. When everyone else is running around talking about their woes, a few folks will say, "Just what I've been waiting for! This is my time to prosper!"

The attitude of turning stress into success is what brought David to the forefront of his nation. It's the ingredient that set him apart from the rest of the nation and eventually made him king. That nation's greatest enemy set David apart from the crowd and launched him into his ministry.

7

Spiritual Warfare

Jesus said, **"And from the days of John the Baptist until now the kingdom of heaven suffers violence, and the violent take it by force" (Matthew 11:12).** If you want the blessing and the benefits of the kingdom of God, you must take them by force!

There are two spiritual kingdoms at work in the earth today: the kingdom of God and the kingdom of the devil. These two kingdoms are very real, and they are all around us right now. Both kingdoms are suffering violence. Both are aggressively, violently going after people. The kingdom of the devil is attempting to consume our world with compromise, evil, and negativity. He's aggressively attacking in the area of politics, social life, and in family life. In all these areas, the devil is trying to possess the lives of people and he's making some progress in many cases.

At the same time, the kingdom of God is violently pressing forward, attempting to possess the lives of people who will walk with God. He is trying to establish righteousness, to establish the blood covenant, to establish the blessing of God in their lives.

Whichever kingdom you side with will affect your life. If you fight to hang on to your old ways of thinking—your television programs, your worldly music, your loose morals—the kingdom of the devil will control your life even as a Christian. He will keep depression, poverty and disease upon you. He will bring divorce into your home and tear your family apart. The kingdom of the devil will force these things on you unless you fight for the kingdom of God.

Jesus said the kingdom of God suffers violence and *the violent take the kingdom by force.* We have to fight for the blessings of the kingdom. We fight to live righteously. It's not easy to be righteous in our world. We fight to be holy and to prosper. It's easier to be poor than it is to prosper. If we're going to stand up for God, we have to be ready to fight.

We have to fight to establish Christian schools. It would be easier to let the devil train our kids. But we fight to establish Christian schools so our children can have a place to learn what is righteous. If we are not taking the kingdom of God by force, we are allowing evil to continue to affect and control our lives. If we are not willing to fight for excellence, then we will live far below God's plan for our lives.

Spiritual warfare is part of our fight for excellence. Spiritual warfare is taking place every day of our lives. We are all involved in one way or another.

"Be sober, be vigilant; because your adversary the devil walks about like a roaring lion, seeking whom he may devour.

Resist him, steadfast in the faith, knowing that the same sufferings are experienced by your brotherhood in the world.

But may the God of all grace, who called us to His eternal glory by Christ Jesus, after you have suffered a while, perfect, establish, strengthen, and settle you.

To Him be the glory and the
dominion forever and ever. Amen."
I Peter 5:8-11

The word "sober" in the Greek text
literally means to "abstain from wine, be
discreet and watch." It means to abstain
from anything that would distract you or
dull your senses; to be watchful and discreet.
"Vigilant" means to be on guard, keep the
vigil, to be aware. It means to rise up, stand
up.

I Peter 5:8-9 in the Amplified Bible reads,
**"Be well balanced (temperate, sober of
mind), be vigilant and cautious at all times;
for that enemy of yours, the devil, roams
around like a lion roaring [in fierce
hunger], seeking someone to seize upon
and devour. Withstand him; be firm in
faith [against his onset—rooted,
established, strong, immovable, and
determined], knowing that the same
(identical) sufferings are appointed to your
brotherhood (the whole body of
Christians) throughout the world."**

Every Christian faces the same fight, the
same battles. We need to realize that it's not
because of our lack of faith that we have this
battle before us—it's *because* we have faith!

The devil is attacking us *because of it*, and we have to use our faith to resist him. Be firm in faith, rooted, established, strong, immovable and determined. That kind of attitude wins battles. The people who pray, "If it be Thy will," don't win many battles. We are to resist the devil, not submit to him.

Some Christians are confused when evil comes. They wonder if God is causing it to happen. Cancer comes and they think God gave it to them to humble them. An accident happens and they believe God did it to teach some kind of a lesson. Divorce comes and they wonder if the Lord broke up their home to try to make them stronger.

If we believe God is bringing these negative, evil things, then it's easy for the devil to defeat us because we think God is our enemy. The devil has sown this lie into the church, *knowing* that if he could get us to believe evil came from God, we would simply lie down and wait to be devoured!

If you will stand up and resist the devil, he will begin to tremble and will flee from your life! But if he thinks you are like the average weak Christian who is going to say, "Well, maybe this is God," he will come and destroy you. Do what the Bible says: be firm in faith, rooted, established, strong, immovable and determined, and the devil will flee, trembling.

Don't be discouraged when problems aren't solved instantaneously. It's *because of your faith* that you do have problems. If you didn't have any faith in God, you wouldn't be a problem for the devil. But since you are believing God, standing up as a witness to the grace of Jesus, talking to people about coming to church and knowing the Lord, that makes you the devil's public enemy number one! The enemy wants to get rid of you! He attacks because you are using your faith. Keep using it, resist him, and win the battle!

The Weapons of the Enemy

The enemy uses many weapons to devour Christians. These are some of the obvious ones: sickness, poverty, sin, divorce, and accidents. We know these are tools of the enemy. We recognize them as attacks of the enemy, so it's easy to fight them. But there are other attacks of the enemy that are more dangerous because they are more subtle. They include depression, fear, worry, and doubt.

When fear comes, we don't always realize that it is an evil spirit. The Bible says

God didn't give us a spirit of fear, but we can accept fear as a normal part of our lives. We make it "okay" to be afraid, to worry, to doubt the Bible. These are the subtle attitudes that weaken the Christian soldier and keep us from fighting for excellence.

Apathy is another subtle attack. The attitude of "Let someone else do it," or "I don't care," keeps us from fighting for excellence in our homes, in our churches and in our life. It causes us to accept mediocrity instead of demanding excellence. Apathy is a dangerous tool of the devil

Another subtle attack is that of "hurt." We usually sympathize and feel sorry for people who are hurt. But we need to realize that "hurt" is just a nice word for "hate." We can't say, "I hate you," so instead we say, "You hurt me." Saying this gives us the right to treat each other as if we hated each other. We can talk about each other; we can reject each other; or we can leave each other. We can do all the things we do when we hate, and it's acceptable. All the while, the devil is sowing seeds of discord and strife in the people involved.

Have you noticed that hurt people often flock together? They're a dangerous flock because they all have the "right" to do whatever they want, because they have been hurt by other people. They are gathering around the "hurt." Hurt can be a spiritual covering for wanting to stay angry at people. It turns into a root of bitterness and the Bible says the root of bitterness brings many troubles.

The Bible says the devil is the most subtle beast in the field. It's his quiet attacks that we must guard against to make sure we don't let evil weaken our fight of faith and our ability to go for excellence.

Warfare Is a Lifestyle

Spiritual warfare has too often been thought of as some heavy, deep, mystical thing. We think, "Spiritual warfare? I know I'm not called to that!"

Everyone is involved with spiritual warfare every day. Spiritual warfare is a way of living, a way of thinking, a way of talking, a way of believing. Spiritual warfare involves praying against evil and binding the enemy.

We are soldiers in the army of the Lord. We feel the anointing of God, and that anointing drives us to fight. We pray, "Devil, take your spirit of murder out of this city. In the name of Jesus, you're not going to kill our babies or our old people. You spirits of murder—go in the name of Jesus! Devil, we're going to heal the sick and raise the dead. You're not going to possess them with your disease. We bind you in Jesus' name!"

Spiritual warfare is a way of living. The apostle Paul wrote, **"I have fought the good fight, I have finished the race, I have kept the faith" (II Timothy 4:7).** Are you fighting spiritual warfare so when you come to the end of your course, you can say to God, "I have fought a good fight?" Or, when you die, will you feel badly about all the things you have never done?

Spiritual warfare is a way of thinking. Paul said, **"For though we walk in the flesh, we do not war according to the flesh. For the weapons of our warfare are not carnal but mighty in God for pulling down strongholds, casting down arguments and every high thing that exalts itself against the knowledge of God, bringing every thought into captivity to the obedience of Christ" (II Corinthians 10:3-5).** "Imaginations" is a Greek word also translated as "reasonings" or "thoughts." Spiritual warfare is a way of thinking. We fight the thoughts of the devil in our minds every day. If we lose the battle in the arena of our minds, we've lost the battle of spiritual warfare.

We must fight the negative thoughts. We must guard our minds from the challenges and input that are contrary to the scriptures. If we accept negativity as normal and begin to think worldly thoughts, we will begin to accept those thoughts and worldly ideas. The spiritual warfare will be over. We must keep casting down the vain imaginations the devil wants to sow in our minds.

Spiritual warfare is a way of talking. **"Death and life are in the power of the tongue..." (Proverbs 18:21).** The tongue is a weapon for spiritual warfare. God knows it and the devil also knows it. Remember the old saying from World War II: "The slip of a lip could sink the ship?" The crews on submarines were put on "silence" to sneak by the enemy under water without being detected. Radar could pick up the sound of their talking, and if detected, the enemy would shoot torpedoes at the sound. If any crew member "slipped their lip" one time, the whole ship could be destroyed. Christians can let their lips slip too much.

We need to remember that death and life are in the power of our tongues. We have what we say according to Jesus (Mark 11:23), be it good or evil.

Spiritual warfare is a way of believing. **"Fight the good fight of <u>faith</u>" (I Timothy 6:12).** We have to fight with faith. Having faith doesn't mean everything will go well. It means we fight no matter how it goes. We need to fight with faith when we feel like being mad, discouraged, or we feel like throwing in the towel. This is when the fight of faith actually starts! Spiritual warfare is believing the best when everything looks bad. Spiritual warfare is to keep on believing in spite of it all.

If Jesus is real in your life then you must also recognize the reality of your enemy. If it took the death of Christ to defeat him, it's going to take some dedication from you to complete that defeat and keep the devil from controlling your life. Jesus has stripped him of his authority, but just like any common criminal, thief, or murderer, he'll do whatever you let him get away with. He can't take your salvation but he can make you a non-effective Christian. The devil doesn't really care if you're saved or not as long as you don't go spreading salvation around. He wants to defeat you in any way that he can.

8
Levels of Spiritual Warfare

The first level of spiritual warfare is fighting temptation and negative thoughts. We briefly touched on this in the last chapter. **"Be sober, be vigilant; because your adversary the devil walks about like a roaring lion, seeking whom he may devour. Resist him, steadfast in the faith..." (I Peter 5:8-9).** Fight temptation and negative thinking. If we can't resist him on this level, we will never make it in the other levels of fighting. If we cannot control our thoughts and resist the temptations, we will never win.

Secondly, we must fight strife in relationships. The enemy wants to use us against one another. We must fight strife. Matthew 12:25 says, **"...Every kingdom divided against itself is brought to desolation...."** Why are there more than

1,000 Christian denominations? Because if we were all united, the devil would be in great trouble! Why does the devil like to have 100 little churches with 50 people in each one? Because they never accomplish very much. But if you get one church with 5,000 people, the whole town knows the church is there and its influence is felt throughout the area.

Why are there as many divorces in Christian homes as there are in the homes of non-Christians? Because the enemy attacks the homes of believers more strongly. If he can divide their homes, he has brought much havoc to the kingdom of God. Demons of strife are working hard so we have to fight for harmony in our relationships.

The third level is to fight with prayer to keep yourself strong in the Lord. **"But you, beloved, building yourselves up on your most holy faith, praying in the Holy Spirit, keep yourselves in the love of God..." (Jude 20-21).** Praying in the Holy Ghost— that's how we stay strong in the Lord. We keep ourselves built up by praying in the Holy Spirit. Rather than talking about the things that worry you, pray in the Holy Ghost.

If we truly believe in spiritual warfare, we will pray in tongues. People who believe that tongues have passed away often believe most of what the devil does has also passed away. They have been deceived on both counts. Praying in tongues is one of our strengths. It keeps our faith strong and we edify ourselves.

The fourth level of spiritual warfare is fighting in prayer for others. Paul said, **"Therefore I exhort first of all that supplications, prayers, intercessions, and giving of thanks be made for all men, for kings and all who are in authority, that we may lead a quiet and peaceable life in all godliness and reverence" (I Timothy 2:1-2).** We need to pray for others. This is where spiritual warfare starts getting exciting. When we are strong, we can resist temptation and strife and keep ourselves built up in the Lord. Then we can forget about ourselves and start praying for others. This is where the majority of our prayer time really should be spent.

Most people spend their time praying for themselves. We should get to the point where we don't have to pray for ourselves anymore. We keep ourselves built up by praying in the Spirit, but then we pray for other people. We begin to call out to God for their lives, for their prosperity, for their healing. Instead of needing a blessing, we become a blessing.

I intercede for people by praying that they will prosper, be wise, and be led of the Spirit. I pray that prayer many times each week. I say, "Lord, I pray over every person in our congregation. I believe, in the Name of Jesus they will be led of the Spirit today. I confess no evil shall come nigh them, no plague shall come nigh their dwelling. I pray, Father, that You'll prosper the work of their hands. I pray they will have the will of God done in their lives."

The fifth level of spiritual warfare is intercession and travail. This is simply a deeper level of number four. Paul said, **"My little children, for whom I labor in birth again until Christ is formed in you..." (Galatians 4:19).** Ezekiel says that God is seeking for those who will intercede and stand in the gap for others. Intercession literally means "to take the place of another."

There are times when we pray for others and there will be an anointing of the Spirit— a flow of the Spirit. We know we're not simply praying for someone else but have actually stepped into their place. God is using us to bring salvation, healing, deliverance or protection to them. We are actually pulling down strongholds for them. And by the power of the Spirit, we are doing it right then in their lives.

The word "travail" has to do with giving birth or bringing forth. We are bringing forth their healing, their deliverance or whatever is needed at the time. This doesn't happen all the time, but it should be a regular part of our prayer life. We are not just praying what we think or know about, or just going through our daily prayer routines. But God begins to step in and we realize there is something more happening. The Lord is using us to intercede and travail for another individual.

If we are praying and interceding for others regularly, then the Holy Ghost can use us at those special times to travail and bring forth the miracle. The real spiritual battle will then come to an end and we will have the victory!

9

The Weapons of Our Warfare

Anyone going into battle knows they will need proper weapons and armor. God told us to fight and He provided us with all the tools we would need to win the battle. But we have to use these tools in order for them to work. If we don't have our armor on, we're easy prey for the devil.

"Finally, my brethren, be strong in the Lord and in the power of His might. Put on the whole armor of God, that you may be able to stand against the wiles of the devil. For we do not wrestle against flesh and blood..." Ephesians 6:10-12). It's not your mother, father, boss, or your neighbor who has become the problem. It's not people who are the problem. Here's what is really happening: **"For we do not wrestle against flesh and blood, but against principalities,**

against powers, against the rulers of the darkness of this age, against spiritual hosts of wickedness in the heavenly places" **(Ephesians 6:12).** Focus your battle in the right direction.

"Therefore take up the whole armor of God, that you may be able to withstand in the evil day" (Ephesians 6:13). We need the *whole armor*. We have to put on the *whole armor* or there will be places left open in our lives where the devil can come in to destroy. What good does it do to lock all of the windows if the front door is left open?

What's the *evil day*? It's any day that evil comes against us. When evil comes against our children, they need to be strong. When evil comes against our marriages, we have to be strong. The *whole armor of God* is what it takes to stand.

"Stand therefore, having girded your waist with truth, having put on the breastplate of righteousness,

And having shod your feet with the preparation of the gospel of peace;

Above all, taking the shield of faith with which you will be able to quench all the fiery darts of the wicked one.

And take the helmet of salvation, and the sword of the Spirit, which is the word of God;

Praying always with all prayer and supplication in the Spirit, being watchful to this end with all perseverance and supplication for all the saints—"

Ephesians 6:14-18

Let's take a look at the armor. *First, gird your loins with truth.* Your loins signify your midsection or your belly. The spirit of man is the belly—it's the core of your life. The center of your life must be girded with truth. A belt of truth protects your inner man— your core—your heart. The core of your life must be anchored to the truth. That truth becomes armor, and when the devil comes, you always have the truth in which to fight. What did Jesus do when the devil came? He said, **"It is written...."** The devil tempted Him again and He said, **"It is written..."** **(Matthew 4:4, 7, 10).**

Many of you can't say, "It is written," because you don't believe the truth or know it. If you have your loins—the core of your life—girded with the truth, the devil has a hard time getting to you. He has no way to bind you because you stand on the truth and the truth makes you free.

Secondly, Paul said to have on the breastplate of righteousness. Your heart is protected by right standing with God. That right standing comes in two ways. One, we are made righteous through faith in Christ. Two, we live righteously by obeying the scripture. I am <u>made</u> righteous because Jesus, who knew no unrighteousness, was made to be sin for me. But I also <u>live</u> righteously because I want to obey the scriptures. That is what guards my heart.

If you're not living right when the enemy attacks, thoughts like this start coming: "I guess I deserved it," or "I guess I let it happen." Or you may think, "My prayers aren't strong enough to stop it because I know I haven't prayed enough." All of these kinds of thoughts come when you are not standing in the righteousness of God. You have to know you're righteous because of your faith in Christ, but you also have to know you're righteous because you're living right.

Next, our feet must be shod with the preparation of the gospel of peace. We are going to spread peace, not gossip. We are going to bring good news, not bad news. We are motivated to share life, not death. We are to spend our time sharing what good things God has done, not bragging about what the devil has done. Our focus in life is to share the gospel of peace.

Paul then tells us that above all we are to take the shield of faith. Faith believes the Word in spite of every circumstance. Faith believes in what God says even when everything else looks contrary.

My faith is in the Word of God, not in what I've seen, felt or experienced. My faith is strong in the Word. When my child has a fever and a runny nose, I hold up the shield of faith and say, "With His stripes—the stripes of Jesus Christ—we are healed." That temperature has to go because my shield of faith quenches all the fiery darts of the wicked one.

If you wonder if healing really works, you will get a fiery dart right between your eyes! That happens to so many people and they wonder why the devil wins. They wonder why bad things keep happening even though they are Christians. They put their shields down when they say, "Do you think this Bible stuff really works?" That's when the darts start flying. When problems come, don't start wondering if the Bible is really true. When problems come, keep the shield of faith up and quench the fiery darts of the wicked one.

Paul said to keep on the helmet of salvation. Keep your mind on your relationship with God. You are a new creature in Christ. You've been saved by the blood of Jesus. You're no longer an old sinner, you're a child of God. **"But as many as received Him, to them He gave the right to become children of God..." (John 1:12).** That's the helmet of salvation!

Next we are to take the sword of the Spirit which is the Word of God. We have to pull that sword out of the sheath daily. We don't win wars by carrying around a sword in a sheath. We win wars by pulling that sword out and using it. Let the enemy see that sword. Flash it in his face. Too often we leave our swords in our pockets. We believe the Bible but we never use it. If we will speak the Word daily, the sword of the Spirit will be piercing through every attack of the enemy.

As you get out of bed say, **"This is the day the Lord hath made. I will rejoice and be glad in it!"** The demons of depression and despair will have to flee. Begin to say, **"Greater is He that is in me. I will rejoice before Thy throne."** Instead of being comfortable with those demons, resist them—fight them. The sword of the Spirit will drive them out of your house.

This is the armor God has given us. If we will use it, we will prosper. Don't be so foolish as to think that you can live day after day not using your armor or not standing against the wiles of the devil. We will be attacked by the enemy and will be destroyed.

God has given us three other main weapons for our spiritual warfare. *Our first weapon is the Name of Jesus.*

The Lord himself told us that no man can come to the Father but through Jesus, for Jesus is **the** way, **the** truth and **the** life (John 14:6). He's not one of many ways, as the New Agers, Buddhists, or Hindus would tell us. He is **THE** way, **THE** truth and **THE** life. No man comes to the Father but by Him.

> **"Therefore God also has highly exalted Him and given Him the name which is above every name,**
>
> **That at the name of Jesus every knee should bow, of those in heaven,**

and of those on earth, and of those under the earth,

And that every tongue should confess that Jesus Christ is Lord, to the glory of God the Father."

Philippians 2:9-11

The New King James version says God has given Him "the" name. The Greek literally says "has given Him the name which is above every name."

There was a special name reserved in heaven. There was a special position and authority reserved in heaven for the Conqueror—for the King of all kings and the Lord of all lords. Jesus received that name. The Father gave Him that place in the universe and in eternity and it will never be taken from Him. At that name every knee shall bow!

Every knee shall bow—one way or another. Those who bow as an act of submission, worship and love to the Lord Jesus Christ, are saved. Those who continue to resist and rebel will bow to Him after they die, or after the judgment as an act of obedience and under the sword of the angels.

Notice something else he said: those in heaven, those in earth, and those under the earth will also bow. Every angel bows to the name of Jesus for He has a more excellent ministry than angels. Every person on earth will bow to the name of Jesus. And every demon, those under the earth, will bow to the name of Jesus. There are no creatures in the spirit world or the natural world with any higher authority. So whether it's an angelic spirit, or human spirit, or a demonic spirit, they will all bow to the name of Jesus.

Jesus said, **"And these signs will follow those who believe: In My name they will cast out demons..." (Mark 16:17).** You and I have authority because He gave us His name as power of attorney. The Lord also said, **"All authority has been given to Me in heaven and on earth. Go therefore and make disciples of all the nations..." (Matthew 28:18-19).** He has invested His power in us. He gave us the right to use His name.

Jesus said whatever you ask when you pray in His name, the Father will give you; in His name you will cast out devils (John l6:23; Mark 16:17). If you pray in His name, you will get answers. Why? Because at His name every knee must bow. This becomes our greatest weapon in spiritual warfare.

This becomes our focus of power when we're coming against evil in our lives.

Here is an example. If we realize that there is a problem in our home, we begin to say, "Father, I pray in the name of Jesus for the comfort of the Spirit, for the peace of the Spirit, for your blessing upon our home." But we don't just talk to the Father. We begin to talk to the enemy that we're warring against. This is important to realize because too often we don't go into battle—we just talk to God about the battle. In Mark 11:23, Jesus said to *say to the mountain* to be removed and cast into the sea. He didn't say to *talk to God about the mountain* —He said to cast it into the sea! If we just talk to God about the mountain, we never get into the battle. The Lord has given you His Name. He gave you the authority. He gave you the weaponry. Don't talk to God about the problem. Get into spiritual warfare and say, "You demons who have come into my house to bring strife, I bind you in the name of Jesus! I cast you out and command you to go!"

There is one last point I want to make clear. I have heard people commanding demons to go to hell. People who pray that way are biblically unaware because the devil and his demons don't have to go to hell yet. Satan's world is the earth. Now you can bind them but you can't send them to hell. Their time has not yet come. Jesus didn't send them to hell. He cast them out, but he didn't send them to hell. You should tell them to leave, and if you want to tell them to go somewhere, tell them to walk in dry places where they will have no influence. They have to obey you. Why? Because you have the Name that is above every name. At that Name, they must go!

Our second weapon is the Word of God. Ephesians 6:17 says the Word of God is the sword of the Spirit. When Satan came to tempt Jesus, how did Jesus respond? He responded with the Word. He didn't come up with His own rationale. He didn't come up with His own philosophies or what some professor or preacher said. He spoke the Word. He said, **"It is written, 'Man shall not live by bread alone, but by every word that proceeds from the mouth of God'"** (Matthew 4:4). **"...it is written, 'You shall worship the LORD your God, and Him only you shall serve'"** (Matthew 4:10). Jesus spoke the Word!

Many people don't know their Bibles, and that's to their detriment. We need to know the Word so we aren't destroyed. The sword of the Spirit comes out of our mouths when we quote the Word. If we don't know the Word, we can't speak it. We need to study, read our Bibles, and listen to powerful teaching so the scriptures become part of our normal way of thinking and speaking. Then when problems come, we naturally speak the Word to them. We don't even have to think about it—it just comes out. What we want is an automatic response of the Word of God working in our lives.

People in the world don't think about what they say. They just curse and tell dirty jokes without thinking about it. People who curse don't realize what they are saying. They have no idea they are speaking so ignorantly. Christians need to be so full of the Word that without thinking, scripture comes out of their mouths.

When a symptom or sickness comes into your home, rather than saying, "Oh, no. How much cough syrup do we have?"—out of your belly comes the sword of the Spirit. "By His stripes we were healed. In the name of Jesus, sickness, I command you to go!"

Our last weapon is prayer.

"Assuredly, I say to you, whatever you bind on earth will be bound in heaven, and whatever you loose on earth will be loosed in heaven.

Again I say to you that if two of you agree on earth concerning anything that they ask, it will be done for them by My Father in heaven."

Matthew 18:18-19

Prayer gives us the authority to bind the work of the devil and loose the work of God.

In Ephesians 6:18, after telling us to be strong in the Lord by putting on the whole armor of God, the apostle ends the passage by saying, **"Praying always with all prayer...."** Prayer is what makes all this armor effective. Prayer is what waves these weapons in the face of the devil. Prayer is what we do with the name of Jesus and the Word of God. Prayer is our greatest weapon.

When we don't pray, we allow demons to crawl into different areas of our lives. The devil has a strategy. He knows our weaknesses and where we could fail. He knows what can be tempting to us. When we don't pray, we let him establish strongholds. That's what Paul called it in II Corinthians 10:4—getting strongholds in certain areas of our lives. Paul said the weapons of our warfare are not carnal but mighty through God to the pulling down of strongholds. We've got to use the weapon of prayer.

Many years ago, my family and I used to go to a little cabin for our summer vacations. It was a rustic cabin that didn't have indoor plumbing. Instead it had a sink with a pipe that went out and drained into the dirt, and a big barrel to catch rain water that would drain down into the kitchen of the cabin. The outhouse was the same. A bucket of water had to be poured down into the toilet in order to flush it.

During the winter, the sink and toilet would become full of spiders. They would crawl up the drain, make their nests and live in there. We would come for vacation and find that the house had been possessed by spiders! We would pour big buckets of water down the pipes to flush all those spiders out. But one thing would consistently happen. As soon as we left, the spiders would start crawling back up. We could come back after one week and the spiders would all be back in full force with their webs spun and their nests built. They had taken over again.

There are demon spirits who are real in the world. They know your weaknesses and where you are tempted. They are familiar with your background. That's why they are called familiar spirits. They crawl into your life to give you recurring problems and difficulties. You go through the same things year after year because you let those demons crawl into your life and influence you. Not that you're demon possessed, but you become oppressed and influenced by these demons.

Prayer washes them out. When you pray strongly, praying with the Word of God and praying in other tongues in faith, it's like pouring a big bucket of water down the sink and washing all those spiders out. But just because you prayed today doesn't mean it will last for a month because those demons are always crawling back, trying to take over again.

10
Accepting the Call
To Battle!

If we went to the streets of America, we would find the majority of people saying they believe the Bible. Most of us were raised to think that the Bible is, for the most part, true.

We have an inner commitment or belief that the Bible is true. And yet when we begin to deal with specific Bible passages, many of us who defend the truth of the Bible begin to back away. If we asked the average person that said he believed in the Bible, "Do you raise your hands and praise the Lord with all that is within you?"—his response could be, "Well, no. In my church we like to be quiet."

"Do you clap your hands and shout to God with a voice of triumph the way the Bible says to praise?"

"Oh, no. That was Old Testament stuff," he might answer.

"Do you believe in the name of Jesus? Do you cast out devils and lay hands on the sick so they will recover?"

He could say, "Oh, no. We have psychologists and doctors now. We don't need that anymore."

"Do you pray in tongues and intercede in the Spirit?"

His answer might be, "Oh no. Those things have passed away. We have universities now and we have education."

When we begin to deal with specific areas that are commanded in the Bible, many of us find excuses and reasons to lay them aside. One of those areas is spiritual warfare. When we begin to talk about the enemy, Satan, demon spirits, and the fact that we really are in a spiritual battle, so many people who say they believe the Bible, rationalize and excuse themselves from great portions of scripture. They have the idea that being a Christian is just going to church, being nice and in a sense, trying to stay out of trouble's way. But in reality, the Bible commands us to get in trouble's way and stop it!

The greatest tool of any army is to convince the enemy there's no problem. The devil has convinced a great many churches that there is no spiritual warfare, there are no devils or demons. Churches are convinced that spiritual warfare is mythology found in archaic writings or the funny thinking of religious fanatics.

Let's let the Bible illustrate that there really is a spiritual enemy, there really is a spiritual war, and that you and I can win that war if we fight it scripturally:

> **"Now the serpent was more cunning than any beast of the field which the LORD God had made. And he said to the woman, "Has God indeed said, 'You shall not eat of every tree of the garden?'"**
>
> **And the serpent said to the woman, "You will not surely die."**
>
> **Genesis 3:1, 4**
>
> **"So Satan answered the LORD and said, 'Does Job fear God for nothing?'**
>
> **Then Satan went out from the presence of the LORD, and struck Job with painful boils from the sole of his foot to the crown of his head."**
>
> **Job 1:9; 2:7**

"How are you fallen from heaven, O Lucifer, son of the morning! How you are cut down to the ground, you who weakened the nations!

For you have said in your heart: 'I will ascend into heaven, I will exalt my throne above the stars of God; I will also sit on the mount of the congregation on the farthest sides of the north;

I will ascend above the heights of the clouds, I will be like the Most High.'

Yet you shall be brought down to Sheol, to the lowest depths of the Pit.

Those who see you will gaze at you, and consider you, saying: 'Is this the man who made the earth tremble, who shook kingdoms,

Who made the world as a wilderness and destroyed its cities, who did not open the house of his prisoners?'"

Isaiah 14:12-17

"You were the anointed cherub who covers; I established you; you were on the holy mountain of God; you walked back and forth in the midst of fiery stones.

You were perfect in your ways from the day you were created, till iniquity was found in you.

By the abundance of your trading you became filled with violence within, and you sinned; therefore I cast you as a profane thing out of the mountain of God; and I destroyed you, O covering cherub, from the midst of the fiery stones.

Your heart was lifted up because of your beauty; you corrupted your wisdom for the sake of your splendor; I cast you to the ground, I laid you before kings, that they might gaze at you.

You defiled your sanctuaries by the multitude of your iniquities, by the iniquity of your trading; therefore I brought fire from your midst; it devoured you, and I turned you to ashes upon the earth in the sight of all who saw you."

Ezekiel 28:14-18

"And these signs will follow those who believe: In My name they will cast out demons; they will speak with new tongues; they will take up serpents...."

Mark 16:17-18

"The thief does not come except to steal, and to kill, and to destroy."

John 10:10

"But even if our gospel is veiled, it is veiled to those who are perishing,

Whose minds the god of this age has blinded, who do not believe, lest the light of the gospel of the glory of Christ, who is the image of God, should shine on them."

II Corinthians 4:3-4

"Put on the whole armor of God, that you may be able to stand against the wiles of the devil.

For we do not wrestle against flesh and blood, but against principalities, against powers, against the rulers of the darkness of this age, against spiritual hosts of wickedness in the heavenly places."

Ephesians 6:11-12

"For the mystery of lawlessness is already at work; only He who now restrains will do so until He is taken out of the way.

And then the lawless one will be revealed, whom the Lord will consume with the breath of His mouth and destroy with the brightness of His coming.

The coming of the lawless one is according to the working of Satan, with all power, signs, and lying wonders...."

II Thessalonians 2:7-9

"Be sober, be vigilant; because your adversary the devil walks about like a roaring lion, seeking whom he may devour.

Resist him, steadfast in the faith, knowing that the same sufferings are experienced by your brotherhood in the world."

I Peter 5:8-9

"And war broke out in heaven: Michael and his angels fought against the dragon; and the dragon and his angels fought,

But they did not prevail, nor was a place found for them in heaven any longer.

So the great dragon was cast out, that serpent of old, called the Devil and Satan, who deceives the whole world; he was cast to the earth, and his angels were cast out with him.

Then I heard a loud voice saying in heaven, 'Now salvation, and strength, and the kingdom of our God, and the power of His Christ have come, for the accuser of our brethren, who accused them before our God day and night, has been cast down.

And they overcame him by the blood of the Lamb and by the word of

their testimony, and they did not love their lives to the death.'"
Revelation 12:7-11

From Genesis to Revelation we find the reality of spiritual battle. It started in the garden of Eden when the serpent lied to Eve and it continues on through the Bible. We know the outcome of the war—Satan will be bound and sent to the pit for eternity. Even knowing this, we must fight the daily battles because the devil will keep trying to discourage God's people from overcoming and sharing in the final victory.

Let's rise up to meet our enemy in battle. Let's accept the call to war and be successful in fighting for excellence for the kingdom of God!

About the Author

Casey Treat is pastor of one of the largest churches in the Pacific Northwest—Christian Faith Center in Seattle, Washington. He also hosts his own daily television program.

Casey is the founder of Dominion College in Seattle and travels extensively each year, speaking at large conventions and churches. His books and teaching-tape series are distributed worldwide.

Casey Treat resides in the Seattle area with his wife, Wendy, and their three children.

Other Books by Casey Treat

Living the New Life

Fulfilling God's Plan For Your Life

Setting Your Course

Errors of the Prosperity Gospel

Renewing the Mind

Reaching Your Destiny

Church Management

Building Leaders That Build A Church

Being Spiritually Minded

Blueprint for Life

Available from:
Christian Faith Center
P.O. Box 98800
Seattle, WA 98198
(206) 824-8188